A Gathering of Old Men

Stage Adaptation based on a novel by Ernest J. Gaines

Written by Gladys W. Muturi

August 24, 2018

LIST OF CHARACTERS

CANDY MARSHALL: a headstrong Caucasian young woman and partial owner of the plantation. She's friends with black plantation including Mathu. She is Lou's girlfriend. She fears that Mathu killed Beau Bouton, but she takes the blame for it.

MATHU: an elderly African American suspected of killing Beau Baton because Beau was killed outside of his house. He cares for Candy like his own daughter and good role model for all the black men.

MAPES: Sheriff of Bayonne. He is good friends with Mathu.

LOU DIMES: Candy's boyfriend. He is a journalist and hopes to marry Candy.

MISS MERLE: owner of a local plantation. She is a kind-hearted woman. She cares for Candy and worries for her.

JACK MARSHALL: Partial owner of the Marshall plantation. Candy's drunken uncle.

BEA MARSHALL: Partial owner of the Marshall Plantation. Candy's aunt.

JANEY: servant of the Marshall House.

FIX BOUTAN: Father of deceased Beau Boutan.

GIL BOUTAN: Brother of deceased Beau Boutan and son of Fix Boutan. After his brother's death, He seeks revenge on Mathu and the other old men on the Marshall Plantation who were responsible. He is a college football star at Louisiana State University.

LUKE WILL: Leads a group of men against the blacks at the Marshall Plantation.

GEORGE "SNOOKUM" ELIOT, JR.: a curious, disobedient, and questioning eleven-year-old boy. He represents the generation of black males that is to come in the future.

GLO HERBERT: Snookum's grandmother.

CAL: Gil's only black friend and teammate in Louisiana State University.

SULLY: Gil and Cal football teammate and friend in Louisiana State University.

CLAUDE: Gil's brother and Fix's son.

AUGUSTE: Fix's brother.

TEE JACK: bar owner.

HERMAN: the coroner.

MARSHALL PLANTATION OLD MEN

CLATOO

JOHNNY PAUL

REVEREND JAMESON

CHARLIE

MAT

DIRTY RED

BILLY WASHINGTON

GABLE

TUCKER

YANK

JACOB

ROOSTER

BING AND DING LEJEUNE

Luke Will's Friends

LEROY

SHARP

ALCEE

HENRY

ROBERT

ACT ONE

SETTING:

Louisiana Cane Farm area; Mathu’s house

TIME:

1970S

OPENING

(CAJUN HARMONICA MUSIC playing in the Background. Curtain opens. A sound of tractor in the background. Big CHARLIE dash enters.)

BEAU (O.S)
I'M GONNA GET YOU CHARLIE BOY!

(CHARLIE scurry enters in Mathu's house. A spotlight on CLATOO standing CENTER STAGE. Everything is silent. CLATOO starts to speak.)

CLATOO
It didn't start this morning. It started about 30 or 40 years ago, when our dear friend Big Charlie boy was on the run. On the run from mister Beau Boutan. Beau was a horrible man. If you look back then, the Boutan family were known household name. Everything that Boutan has done, we black folks get framed, most likely to get lynch, beaten, women getting raped, name calling us, "Nigger this, Nigger that". Well, that was then, this is now. Charlie was getting chased by Beau, Fix's son, driving in his tractor with a loaded shotgun. When Beau tried to find him….

(A sound of GUN SHOT FIRED. BACKGROUND MUSIC stops playing. Another SPOTLIGHT on the DEAD BODY of BEAU BOUTAN, covered with a long, white sheet smear with his blood on the ground. CLATOO stares at the body for a dramatic second then continues the story.)

CLATOO
Shots fired outside of Mathu's House and Beau was dead. How's Fix gonna feel now if he finds his son shot dead by a black man outside of his home? What will be the outcome? What has the world come into? What do you think?

(BLACKOUT. END OF OPENING.)

ACT ONE

SCENE ONE

SETTING: Louisiana; Outside of Glo's House

AT RISE: Light Fades on. It's the 1970s at Louisiana. SNOOKUM, 11, sitting on the porch tossing his football up and down on the porch outside of his house. A sound of a car arriving at the house. Car stops and someone ejecting out of the car.

CANDY (O.S)
Aunt Glo, Oh, Aunt Glo, Oh, Aunt Glo.

(SNOOKUM hears a VOICE and looks around to find the voice. AUNT GLO HERBERT, Snookum's grandmother enters and sees SNOOKUM on the porch.)

AUNT GLO
Snookum, what are doing out here? I thought I told you go and finish your turnips.

SNOOKUM
But I don't like turnips.

AUNT GLO
Did I ask if you like them?

CANDY (O.S)
Aunt Glo, Oh, Aunt Glo.

(SNOOKUM hears the VOICE again and starts the find the voice.)

AUNT GLO
(to Snookum)
Boy, Is your name, Aunt or Glo? Get back in that house.

SNOOKUM
Yes, Gram Mon.

(SNOOKUM enters in the house. AUNT GLO looks to see who's calling her. CANDY MARSHALL, short haircut, wearing a white shirt and blue jeans with a black belt and brown boots enters. AUNT GLO sees CANDY.)

CANDY
(looking for Glo)
Oh, Aunt Glo, Oh, Aunt Glo.

AUNT GLO
(to Candy)
Candy? What is it?

CANDY
Snookum in there?

AUNT GLO
Yes, he's at the table eating.

ANUT GLO (CONT'D)
What's the matter, Candy?

CANDY
Get Snookum out here.

AUNT GLO
Why? Did Snookum did something wrong?

CANDY
Aunt Glo, we ain't got the time. Get Snookum out here.

AUNT GLO
(calling Snookum from the door)
Snookum! Come on out here!

(SNOOKUM enters out the house.)

AUNT GLO
(to Snookum)
Candy wants to talk to you.

(AUNT GLO exit.)

SNOOKUM
(to Candy)
Hey, Candy, what is it?

CANDY
Come here, Snookum.

(SNOOKUM comes closer to CANDY. She leans in with SNOOKUM.)

CANDY
Now, listen. I want you to run, and I don't want you to stop running. I want you to go tell Rufe and Reverend Jameson and Corrine and the rest of them to gather at Mathu's house right away. And I want you to go to the front, and I want you to-listen to me good, now.

(CANDY puts her hands-on SNOOKUM's shoulders.)

CANDY

Go up to the house and see if Miss Merle's there. If she is, tell her I say come quick. No, if she's there, tell her to call Lou and tell Lou to come quick. Both of them, to come here quick. If she's not, tell Janey to call her and Lou to get here quick. Don't waste time on the phone talking, just get here quick. Don't do nothing just get here quick. You heard what I said, Snookum? Go!

SNOOKUM

What I'm telling all them people to get here quick for?

(CANDY lets go of SNOOKUM.)

CANDY

That's not your concern, Snookum. You're nothing but a little boy. Now, get moving and don't stop running. Go!

(SNOOKUM scurries exit. BLACKOUT. END OF SCENE ONE.)

ACT ONE

SCENE TWO

SETTING: Outside of Mathu's House

AT RISE: Outside of Mathu's House, a sound of tractor engine is on and running. The dead body of BEAU BOUTAN, a white farmer laying on STAGE LEFT. SNOOKUM scurries enter from STAGE RIGHT. He stops and sees the dead body. He tries to look under the sheets. MATHU enters, grey-white beard, dressed in a white undershirt, black dress pants, straw hat and a shot gun in his hand.

MATHU
(yelling at Snookum)
HEY!

(SNOOKUM alarmed by MATHU'S voice.)

MATHU (CONT'D)
Get away from there boy!

(SNOOKUM slowly backs away from the body but couldn't stop looking at BEAU'S motionless dead body.)

MATHU
What's the matter you? Never seen a dead body before.

SNOOKUM
(nods)
No.

SNOOKUM (CONT'D)
I'm doing something for Candy.

MATHU
You ain't doing nothing for her there. Now get away from there.

(MATHU comes closer to the dead body. He squats down to check on the body, feeling no remorse at all.)

SNOOKUM
Candy want everybody at your house.

MATHU
If that's what she wants, you better go on and do it.

(SNOOKUM hears the tractor motor is running.)

SNOOKUM
Where's Charlie? How come the motor is running?

MATHU
That's none of your business. Now get out of here or I'll whoop your ass. Go on! Now! Go!

(SNOOKUM scurries exit. MATHU watches as SNOOKUM leaves.)

MATHU
(calling Charlie from his house)
Charlie? Come on out here.

(A frightened CHARLIE, in his 60'S, chubby, all sweaty, wearing a dirty torn undershirt and blue overalls breathing heavily enters out MATHU's house. MATHU takes out his cigarette from his pocket and starts to smoke.)

CHARLIE
(panic)
We dead Mathu! We dead!

MATHU
(blows out a smoke)
Oh, Hush up, you old fool.

MATHU (CONT'D)
What's done is done.

CHARLIE
I ain't gonna stay here, Mathu. Wait and until Fix finds out what happened to his son, Beau.

CHARLIE (CONT'D)
He gonna kill us. Better yet lynch us.

(CHARLIE looks at the dead body. MATHU continues to smoke on his cigarette.)

CHARLIE
Killed by somebody black? I just can't stay with you.

MATHU
Go on, then! Get!

(CHARLIE is about to leave but then stops and plea with MATHU.)

CHARLIE
I can't stay here, Mathu. I, I, I ca-.

CHARLIE (CONT'D)
(emotional)
They'll hang me. I know it. They'll jus-. They'll hang me.

(A SOUND of a car approaching near MATHU'S House. MATHU and CHARLIE hears and sees a car coming.)

CHARLIE
(scared)
Oh, God! They're coming now!

MATHU
(to Charlie)
Go on! Get!

(CHARLIE scurries exit. MATHU starts to load his gun. A sound of car ejects. He checks to see whose coming. CANDY MARSHALL enters. MATHU stops loading the gun and puts it down. CANDY sees the body. She couldn't keep her eyes off BEAU's dead body.)

CANDY
(to Mathu)
Mathu, I want you to answer me.

(MATHU looks at CANDY.)

MATHU
What?

CANDY
Did you do this? Did you kill Beau? You know this is Fix's son?

(MATHU looks at the dead body and says nothing to CANDY.)

CANDY
Mathu, you answer me! Did you do this? Yes or No?

(MATHU sits down with his gun by his side and continues to smoke.)

MATHU
Would you be mad if I did it?

(CANDY comes closer to MATHU.)

CANDY
(concern)
I'm afraid for you, Mathu. You know what's gonna happen if Fix finds out about this.

MATHU

Humph….and you had that Snookum boy to get everyone to come here?

CANDY

Yes, I had to. I had to tell Snookum to get everyone here.

CANDY (CONT'D)

Mathu, you're the only person that's been there for me. I can't imagine living without you. That's not just any white man lying out there.

CANDY

Mathu, please. I can't let him kill you.

(MATHU stays silent. BLACKOUT. END OF SCENE TWO.)

ACT ONE

SCENE THREE

SETTING: Outside of Marshall House

AT RISE: SNOOKUM feeling exhausted from all that running enters.

SNOOKUM
(pant)
Janey….Janey.

SNOOKUM (CONT'D)
Janey! Janey! Janey!

(JANEY enters from the Marshall House carrying a basket of clean linen laundry.)

JANEY
What's the matter with you, boy? Don't you know the Major and Miss Bea in there trying to sleep.

SNOOKUM
Candy sent me.

JANEY
She tell you to wake up the dead, did she? What's the matter with you?

SNOOKUM
Candy want you to call Lou.

(JANEY starts to fold the laundry.)

JANEY
You say "Mr. Lou" and you say "Miss Candy". I don't care how libbel they is, you still a child. You say mister and miss round me. You ain't too old for me to tan your butt, you know.

SNOOKUM
Miss Merle in there?

JANEY
No, she ain't.

SNOOKUM
Candy sent me here to tell you to call Lou and Miss Merle. And tell them to come right away at Mathu's.

JANEY
Why? What Candy want with them in the quarters?

SNOOKUM

Something to do with Mathu and Beau. Beau laying on his back at Mathu's yard. And Mathu squatting there with that shotgun.

(JANEY is in shock and stops what she is doing.)

JANEY

(shock)

What? Oh, my Lord! Oh Lord! That gunshot…That shot I heard. Oh Lord!

(JANEY takes the laundry basket and enters inside the Marshall House.)

SNOOKUM

Janey, you getting me some tea cakes?

(JANEY enters out of the Marshall House.)

JANEY

(raising her hand getting ready to smack Snookum)

Tea ca-Boy!

(SNOOKUM jerks away from JANEY.)

SNOOKUM

Well, can at least get some water? Candy didn't pay me enough to go around to tell everyone to come at Mathu's.

JANEY

Fine.

(JANEY enters back inside the Marshall House. Then, she enters out with a glass of water and a bag of teacakes.)

JANEY

(hands water to Snookum)

Here! Take it!

SNOOKUM

Thanks!

(SNOOKUM drinks the water.)

JANEY

Hurry up! Before, Mister and Miss Marshall wakes up.

(SNOOKUM finishes his water and gives the empty glass to JANEY.)

JANEY
(gives Snookum a bag of teacakes)
Here!

SNOOKUM
(takes the bag)
Thanks, Janey!

(SNOOKUM runs to exit.)

JANEY
(worried)
Oh, Lord! Jesus, Oh, Lord! Lord have Mercy!

(BLACKOUT. END OF SCENE THREE.)

ACT ONE

SCENE FOUR

SETTING: Outside of Marshall House

AT RISE: JACK MARSHALL, partial owner of the plantation, is sitting on his rocking chair smoking on a pipe, next to him, an ice empty glass on a small table.

JACK
Janey, Janey. Get over here.

(JANEY enters from the Marshall House.)

JANEY
(gloomy)
Yessir.

JACK
(holding out his glass)
Get me another drink.

(JANEY takes the glass.)

JANEY
(gloomy)
Yessir.

(JANEY exits to the Marshall House. JACK continues to sit on his rocking chair while resting his eyes. MISS MERLE enters with a fresh baked apple pie in her hands.)

MISS MERLE
Good Afternoon, Jack.

JACK
(half-awake)
Huh, uh, Afternoon, Miss Merle. What brings you here?

MISS MERLE
Just thought I stopped by and drop off this. Lucy and I baked some fresh apple pies for you.

JACK
Is that so?

(JACK glance at the pie.)

JACK
Oh, is this for me?

MISS MERLE
What do you think?

(JANEY enters with a glass of burgundy gives it to JACK, not looking at MISS MERLE.)

MISS MERLE
Jack, isn't too early for you to drink liquor. For god sake, it's the afternoon.

(JACK grunt ignores MISS MERLE and continues to drink. MISS MERLE sees JANEY.)

MISS MERLE
Janey!

(JANEY sees MISS MERLE.)

JANEY
(surprised)
Miss Merle!

MISS MERLE
You didn't see me.

JANEY
Oh, I'm sorry.

(MISS MERLE notices JANEY's eyes.)

MISS MERLE
(looking into Janey eyes)
Have you been crying?

JANEY
No, no, Miss Merle.

MISS MERLE
Seems you have been crying.

JANEY
(trying not to cry)
Oh, I'm not crying. Its jus-, just the onions. I was chopping some onions for dinner. I, I, been calling and calling your house.

MISS MERLE
I was on my way over here. What's the matter? What happened?

JANEY
Candy…

MISS MERLE
What about Candy?

JANEY
They been killing.

MISS MERLE
(concern)
What? Candy?

JANEY
No ma'am, Beau.

MISS MERLE
Beau? What happened? Who got killed?

JANEY
Beau. Beau's dead.

MISS MERLE
What? Oh, my God! Where's Candy?

JANEY
In the quarters.

MISS MERLE
What's she doing down there?

JANEY
That's where it happened. Outside at Mathu's house.

MISS MERLE
(shocked)
Oh, my God! Oh, my God!

(MISS MERLE sees JACK asleep in his rocking chair.)

MISS MERLE
(trying to wake up Jack)
Jack? Jack? Jack, wake up!

JANEY
He ain't listening to you.

MISS MERLE

It's obvious because you gave him too much to drink. He's too drunk to listen to me. Oh, to hell with him. He never wanted any part of it anyhow.

MISS MERLE (CONT'D)

(to Janey)

Who else know about this?

JANEY

Just the people in the quarters. She wanted me to notify you and Mr. Lou, but nobody else.

MISS MERLE

You got Lou?

JANEY

He's at a meeting.

MISS MERLE

Shit.

MISS MERLE (CONT'D)

Where's Bea?

JANEY

She's in the back picking some pecans.

(BEA MARSHALL enters with a bucket filled with pecans.)

BEA

(to Janey)

Janey, can put these pecans in the kitchen for me.

(BEA hands JANEY the bucket.)

JANEY

(takes the bucket)

Yes ma'am.

BEA

And can you get me a pea picker. It's hot out here!

JANEY

Yes ma'am.

(BEA sees MISS MERLE.)

BEA

Miss Merle, what brings you here? I didn't invite you here.

(BEA looks at MISS MERLE's pie on her hands.)

BEA
Apple pie? Why did you bring apple pie? You know I don't like apple pie.

MISS MERLE
The pie is not for you, Bea. It's for Jack.

BEA
Oh.

MISS MERLE
And there's no time for peapickers. Beau Bouton is dead.

BEA
Who?

MISS MERLE
Beau Bouton, Fix's son. He's dead.

BEA
And?

MISS MERLE
He's lying there dead at Mathu's yard. And Candy is down there as well.

(JANEY enters from the house with a tray of two glass of peapickers. BEA sees JANEY with drinks.)

BEA
Oh, yes. Janey, hand me my drink.

MISS MERLE
(stops Janey)
Oh, no, Janey. I need you to go in the kitchen, call Lou and tell him to come to Mathu's immediately.

(JANEY tries to exit in the house.)

BEA
(stops Janey)
Now, wait just a minute, Janey. You know what time it is. Hand it over.

(JANEY stops and tries to hand BEA her pea picker.)

MISS MERLE
(stops Janey)
No, Janey don't you mo-

BEA
(interrupts)
Whoa! Hold on! You told her "Don't"? This is not Seven Oaks, Miss. Here on Marshall Miss, I say "Don't". And I say "Do."

MISS MERLE
You're not listening, Bea. We have a dead Cajun man lying in Mathu's yard.

BEA
And, what do you want me to do about it? People die all the time.

BEA (CONT'D)
(to Janey)
Ok, Janey, what are you waiting for?

(JANEY sighs and finally gives BEA her peapickers.)

BEA
Thank you.

BEA (CONT'D)
It's about time someone shot that bastard.

(JANEY gives JACK a glass of peapickers. JACK'S eyes peek open, he sees the peapickers and takes it.)

MISS MERLE
Ok, listen here, Janey—.

JANEY
Oh, Miss Merle, please, don't make me do nothing like that.

MISS MERLE
Don't you dare tell me not to do nothing like that. Now, I want you to go back in the kitchen, call Lou and tell him to get his butt over here at Mathu's now. Do you understand me?

JANEY
(understood)
Yes, miss.

MISS MERLE
Alright, I'll be back. I'm going to Mathu's to check on Candy.

(MISS MERLE exits.)

BEA
(ignoring Miss Merle)
Humph.

(BEA and JACK toast their peapickers distance from each other and drink their peapickers. BLACKOUT. END OF SCENE FOUR.)

ACT ONE

SCENE FIVE

SETTING: Outside of Mathu's House.

AT RISE: Mathu's friends, JOHNNY PAUL and RUFE are at Mathu's house with their shot guns in their hands.

CANDY
Hey guys!

JOHNNY PAUL & RUFE
Hey Candy!

CANDY
Thank y'all for coming.

(CANDY looks to see if more people are coming at MATHU'S House. MISS MERLE enters from STAGE RIGHT.)

RUFE
Hey, Miss Merle.

MISS MERLE
Hello, boys.

JOHNNY PAUL
Hey, Miss Merle.

MISS MERLE
How you doing?

RUFE
(jokingly)
Miss Merle, is that pie for me? I'm hungry.

MISS MERLE
There's plenty more for everyone, Rufe. I made more for everyone.

(MISS MERLE sees CANDY.)

MISS MERLE
Candy?

CANDY
(surprised)
Miss Merle?

MISS MERLE
I've been willing to talk to you. Why are they all carrying guns? What's going on here?

(MISS MERLE sees BEAU BOUTAN's dead body. She is in shock.)

MISS MERLE
(shock)
Oh my God!

CANDY
Miss Merle, I killed Beau.

MISS MERLE
What?

CANDY
Yeah, I did it, I shot him.

(CANDY grabs MATHU's shotgun.)

CANDY
(holding shotgun)
With this shotgun. Mathu's shotgun. I used Mathu's shotgun to shoot Beau to stop him from bothering my people. But all of sudden Mathu said he shot him. Then, Rufe said he shot him. And, Johnny Paul, out of nowhere, said he shot him. But I'm still the one who shot him.

(MISS MERLE looks at CANDY, then MATHU, RUFE, and JOHNNY PAUL and BEAU's dead body. All the Old Men agreed with CANDY. She puts the gun down.)

MISS MERLE
No!

CANDY
Yes, Miss Merle!

MISS MERLE
No, Candy. I don't believe you.

CANDY
Yes, Miss Merle. I did it. You have to believe me.

MISS MERLE
Don't they know who that is?

CANDY
They know. They just want the credit for shooting him. But I'm the one who shot him.

MISS MERLE
Here in Mathu's yard, Candy? If Mapes comes here and sees this. You know, Mapes is no fool.

(MISS MERLE pulls CANDY aside.)

MISS MERLE
(quietly)
You don't think Mathu could've done this? Do you?

CANDY
Look, I told you before. I shot him. And Mapes is not gonna do a damn thing about it. I need you to believe me. Clinton can handle Mapes in court.

MISS MERLE
And who's going to handle Fix, Candy?

CANDY
I'll take care of it. Believe me. I won't let them touch my people.

MISS MERLE
Candy...

CANDY
Look, I need you to do something for me.

MISS MERLE
Oh, no, Candy.

CANDY
Yes, Miss Merle. I need you to go and get me more people and more twelve-gauge shotguns.

MISS MERLE
Shotguns? And more people for what?

CANDY
You see what they're doing.

MISS MERLE
I see old men with shotguns, I see that.

CANDY
Yes, And I need more. Mapes come here, he'll beat up two till they talk, then he'll take one. I need more people here.

MISS MERLE
Candy, are you crazy? Do you know what you're saying?

CANDY
I know what I am saying, and I know what I'm doing. Get more people here quick. We don't have much time.

MISS MERLE
Get Who?

CANDY
Who?

MISS MERLE
Yes, who, Candy. Who?

CANDY
There's not a black family in this parish Fix and his crowd hasn't hurt sometime or other. You're older than I am, you know that better than I do. Get any of them, get all of them. Now is their chance to stand.

MISS MERLE
And be killed? Is that what you want? Blood all over the place?

CANDY
Look around you, Miss Merle. Aren't they ready to die? Look at Mathu. Do you know who Mathu is, Miss Merle?

MISS MERLE
Yes, I know who Mathu is. I knew Mathu long before you were born.

CANDY
I can't lose Mathu, Miss Merle. He's the only one who raised me since my parents died.

MISS MERLE
And so have I, Candy. I've been there for you too. But you can't protect Mathu like this. Not like this. He needs to own up to his responsibilities.

CANDY

No way, Miss Merle. No way, I won't let him. Now we need to notify Mapes sooner or later. I need you to tell Janey to call Lou-

(CANDY cuts a slice of pie, grabs a napkin, and takes a piece.)

MISS MERLE

I already told Janey to call Lou to come down here.

(CANDY eats a piece of pie.)

CANDY

(mouth full)

You did?

MISS MERLE

Yes.

CANDY

Well, did you ask Janey if she knows anybody who don't like Fix?

MISS MERLE

Well, no. But I'll ask Janey if she knows.

CANDY

So you'll help me?

MISS MERLE

Alright, Alright. I will do it for you.

(CANDY hugs MISS MERLE.)

CANDY

Thank you, Miss Merle.

MISS MERLE

I hope you know what you're doing, Candy.

CANDY

Trust me, I know what I'm doing. Just Hurry, get more people, more twelve-gauge shotguns, and empty shells. We don't have much time.

MISS MERLE

Alright. I'll be back.

(MISS MERLE exit.)

CANDY
(to Mathu)
Well, it's done, Mathu. Can't nothing stop it now.

(BLACKOUT. END OF SCENE FIVE.)

ACT ONE

SCENE SIX

SETTING: Nearby St. Charles River

AT RISE: On STAGE RIGHT, MAT and CHIMLEY are both laughing and fishing by the river. Fishing rods on their hands and their blue and red coolers next to them.

CHIMLEY
Yeah, I remember those times-

SNOOKUM (O.S)
Mat! Chimley!

(MAT and CHIMLEY stops and hears a voice.)

MAT
You hear that? I thought I heard Glo's grandson.

CHIMLEY
I think so. It sounds like him. What's his name?

MAT
Snookum.

CHIMLEY
Snookum! Yeah! That's his name.

(SNOOKUM enters.)

SNOOKUM
Mat! Chimley!

MAT
Snookum. Watchu doin here, boy?

SNOOKUM
Candy sent me to tell both of y'all to come to Mathu's. She also said y'all both need to bring your twelve-gauge shotguns and empty shells.

MAT
All that for what?

CHIMLEY
Why, boy?

SNOOKUM

Got something to do with Mathu. He shot a white man in his yard.

CHIMLEY

White man? Boy, white people have names. Who did he shoot?

SNOOKUM

Mathu shot Beau Boutan, Fix's son.

MAT & CHIMLEY

Beau?

SNOOKUM

Yup.

CHIMLEY

Man, White people sure do know how to ruin a good river. Alright, we'll be right over.

SNOOKUM

Y'all better hurry or unless you want to crawl and hide in your rooms. Me, I've done my part.

(MAT and CHIMLEY exit with their fishing rods and coolers. REVERNED JAMESON enters with a Bible in his hand. SNOOKUM runs and bumps into REVERNED JAMESON.)

SNOOKUM

Excuse me, Reverend.

(REVERNED JAMESON stops SNOOKUM for a minute.)

REVERNED JAMESON

Snookum, where you heading off to? I was going to stop by at your house.

SNOOKUM

I can't talk right now, Reverend. Candy sent me to get everybody at Mathu's. And she wants you to come too.

REVERNED JAMESON

Mathu? Why's everyone going to Mathu's? And why me?

SNOOKUM

Because Mathu shot a white man dead outside of his yard. And Candy sent me to tell you to come to Mathu's.

REVERNED JAMESON

Mathu? Shot who?

SNOOKUM
Beau Boutan.

REVERNED JAMESON
(shocked)
Fix's son.

SNOOKUM
Just come to Mathu's, Reverend. Right now, Candy wants me to go get more people.

(SNOOKUM scurries exit. BLACKOUT. END OF SCENE SIX.)

ACT ONE

SCENE SEVEN

SETTING: Outside of Marshall's House

AT RISE: MISS MERLE enters calling Janey's name. BEA MARSHALL and JACK MARSHALL are sitting in a trance enjoying nice weather.

MISS MERLE
Janey! Janey!

(MISS MERLE knocks on the door.)

MISS MERLE
(knocking)
Janey!

(JANEY opens and peeks the door.)

JANEY
(to Miss Merle)
Yes, Miss.

MISS MERLE
Janey, who you know don't like Fix?

JANEY
Ma'am?

MISS MERLE
Don't answer me with a question, Janey. Just give me an answer.

JANEY
Well, I don't know anybody.

BEA
I don't like Fix. So, beat it. Why ask Janey if she knows who doesn't like Fix?

MISS MERLE
(to Bea)
Oh, Bea, it was horrible. I saw the body and Candy is the one claiming she did it.

BEA
You think she did it?

MISS MERLE
No. But I know for a fact Mathu might've done it.

JANEY
Oh Lord!

MISS MERLE
(to Janey)
Janey. I need call everyone to come to Mathu's.

JANEY
But, who should I call first?

BEA
I know who you should call.

MISS MERLE
(to Bea)
Who?

BEA
Clatoo. You know that gal got spunk like Grandpa Nate.

MISS MERLE
Grandpa Nate?

BEA
My grandpa. Her great-great grandpa. About time she shot one of the Cajuns, messing the land with those tractors. Yes, she got spunk in her. Probably nobody wants to marry her.

MISS MERLE
Beatrice, will you please be quiet for a minute? Tell me about Clatoo and how do we find him.

BEA
Fix and Clatoo have been at each other throats for years. It started when one of Clatoo's sisters stabbed Fix's brother Forest for trying to rape her. She didn't kill him. She, however, ended up in pen. She died in pen. Some say she died of insanity that's what everybody said. That happened before the Second World War.

(MISS MERLE realizes where CLATOO might be.)

MISS MERLE
Janey, Clatoo still at Glenn?

JANEY
Yes, ma'am. Still there, gardening.

MISS MERLE
Has he got a phone?

JANEY
I, I, I, I.

(MISS MERLE grabs JANEY by the dress.)

MISS MERLE
Tell me, dammit.

JANEY
He stay there with Emma.

MISS MERLE
What name Emma goes under?

JANEY
Henderson. I believe-yes, ma'am. It's Henderson.

MISS MERLE
Janey, did you get Lou?

JANEY
Yes, I did, Miss. He's on his way.

MISS MERLE
Oh, good. Make sure tell everyone to come to Mathu's and bring their shotguns.

(MISS MERLE exit.)

BEA
Janey, give me another pea picker.

JANEY
Oh, no, ma'am. Not again.

BEA
Hey, I helped you with the names. You get me another pea picker.

JANEY
Yes, ma'am.

JANEY
(to Jack)
You need anything, sir?

(JACK nods. JANEY exit in the house. END OF SCENE SEVEN.)

ACT ONE

SCENE EIGHT

SETTING: Outside of Mathu's House

AT RISE: Back at Mathu's, Two Men: BILLY WASHINGTON and YANK have arrived at Mathu's with their shotguns sitting on the porch with JOHNNY PAUL and RUFE. MATHU is back inside his home. CANDY is standing on the porch waiting for more people to come.

ELLA (O.S.)
Mat, you ain't hearing me.

MAT (O.S)
Oh, Leave me alone, woman.

(MAT enters with his shotgun. ELLA, Mat's wife enters.)

MAT
Stop following me and get back in the house.

ELLA
Mat, I'm not going anywhere until you tell me something.

(MAT loads his shotgun.)

MAT
Woman, this doesn't involve you. Now, go home and stay there. This is men's business.

ELLA
Well, I'm making it my business.

(ELLA sees BEAU'S DEAD BODY.)

ELLA
What's going on here?

MAT
That's why I don't want you here, woman. Come on.

(MAT pulls away ELLA from the Dead Body.)

MAT
Alright, I'll tell you. A Cajun's dead over here laying in Mathu's yard. Now you know.

ELLA

And what's got to do with you, Mat, you old fool? And what's got to do with these men and their guns?

MAT

You mean you still don't know?

ELLA

Your old fool! Have y'all gone crazy?

MAT

That's right. Anytime we say we go'n stand up for something, they say we crazy. Yes, we all gone crazy, woman.

ELLA

You old fool! If I can't stop you, I bet you I'll call your brother. He'll stop you.

(ELLA starts to walk away.)

MAT

Woman, if you think that you and Jesse are gonna stop me. You better stay out of my way if you know what's good for you.

(ELLA walks back to MAT.)

ELLA

If you think I'm go'n and let you go, get yourself kilt-

MAT

You can't stop me, woman.

ELLA

What's the matter with you, old fool?

MAT

What's the matter with me? What's the matter with me? All these years we've been living together, woman, and you ask me, "What's the matter with me?" The years we done struggled in George Medlow's field, making him richer and richer, and us poorer and poorer and you still don't know what's the matter with me? The years I done stood in that backyard and cussed at God, the years I done stood out on that front Garry and cussed the world, the times I done come home drunk and beat you for no reason at all- and woman, you still don't know what's the matter with me? Oliver, woman! Oliver. May God rest his soul. How they let him die in the hospital because he was black. No doctor to serve him, let him bleed to death, cause he was black. And you ask me what's the matter with me?

MAT (CONT'D)
He works in mysterious ways. Give an old nigger like me one more chance to do something with his life. He gived me that chance, and I'm taking it. I know I'm old and I maybe crazy but I'm staying here fighting.

ELLA
Lord have mercy.

MAT
Pray if you want to. Pray for all us old fools. But woman, don't try and stop me. Ella, I'm done talking you. Now, go on home.

ELLA
Oh, I'm not done talking with you yet, you old fool.

CANDY
Ella, go on home.

ELLA
Candy, you're the one who started this. You better hope and pray nothing happens to my husband.

(ELLA exit.)

CANDY
Thanks for coming, Mat.

MAT
How you doing, Candy?

(MAT greets the MEN.)

MAT
(to Billy Washington)
How you feel, old buddy?

BILLY WASHINGTON
Scared but I'm here.

(CHIMLEY with his gun enters.)

CHIMLEY
(to Billy Washington)
How could you be scared yet you here?

CHIMLEY
Shoot! At least I showed up here. I'm seventy-one years old, I ain't afraid to crawl in my bed.

BILLY WASHINGTON
Oh, hush up, old fool!

YANK
Hey y'all! Y'all don't think Mathu could have done this?

(All MEN look at the dead body.)

MAT
Could be. Could be Mathu.

YANK
What about Candy? Cus Candy says she's the one who did it.

BILLY WASHINGTON
And that's why we here?

MAT
No way! No way! Ain't no way!

CHIMLEY
She's a child.

YANK
She's in her 20s. She ain't no baby.

MAT
You know I remember when Mathu had a fight with Fix. It started over a Coke bottle. After Fix drunk his Coke, he wanted Mathu to take the empty bottle back in the store. Mathu said, "Nah. I ain't nobody's servant." So, Fix ask him again to go take the empty bottle back in the store or fight. A bunch of people including myself were there, white and black, sitting on the garry eating gingerbread and drinking pop. Even Sheriff Guidry was there too. And when Mathu refused again, Fix hit him. And Mathu he fought back. Worst fight I've ever seen. But when it was over, Mathu was up, and Fix was down.

CHIMLEY
Then what happened?

MAT

The white folks wanted to lynch him but the Sheriff stopped them. Sheriff walked up to Mathu and hit him in the jaw. Mathu hit the ground. He turned to Fix and hit in the mouth too. Fix fell and hit the ground.

(MATHU enters from the scene.)

YANK

Hey Mathu!

MATHU

Hey.

(MATHU greets the MEN. MAT takes the cigarette from his ear.)

MATHU

(takes the cigarette back from Mat)

Give me that back. You know you ain't suppose to be smoking.

MAT

Fool, do you think I listen to my wife?

(MATHU chuckles.)

BILLY WASHINGTON

How you been, Mathu?

MATHU

I've been fine.

CHIMLEY

You don't look fine.

(MATHU is silent.)

MATHU

(pointing his shotgun at the dead body)

You see that?

(All the Men look BEAU BONTAN's Dead body.)

MATHU

I killed him. Candy's the one who called y'all here. Not me. When the Sheriff comes, I'm turning myself in.

RUFE

No you ain't. I'm gonna turn myself in to the Sheriff. I'm the one who did it.

MATHU
You ain't taking no credit for what I did.

JOHNNY PAUL
Oh, nah! I'm the one who shot him. It was me.

MAT
No, it wasn't you, Johnny Paul. I took Beau down.

(Shots fire offstage. Everybody ducks.)

MAT
That wasn't me!

BILLY WASHINGTON
No it ain't. Look!

(CLATOO enters with his shotgun and a shoebox filled with bullets, and men including DIRTY RED, ROOSTER, GABLE, TUCKER, JACOB, BING LEJEUNE, and DING LEJEUNE with their shotguns enter.)

MAT
Wait a minute! It's Clatoo!

(All the men greet each other except MATHU.)

MAT
Who was the one who made that shot?

GABLE
Oh, that was Red. He's the one trying to shoot that rabbit.

DIRTY RED
I missed.

(All the men continue to greet each other.)

CANDY
(shaking hands with Clatoo)
Great seeing you, Clatoo.

CLATOO
How you doing, Candy?

CANDY
Fine thanks for coming.

CLATOO
(to Mathu)
How you doing, Mathu?

MATHU
Fine.

(CLATOO starts to look for the DEAD BODY.)

CLATOO
Well, where is he?

(CLATOO sees the DEAD BODY.)

CLATOO
Ah, there he is. Right where I shot him. That's right, I killed him. I did it for my brother.

DIRTY RED
I shot him. I shot him. I'm the one who shot him.

JACOB
I'm gonna turn myself in. I shot Beau. I shot him.

DIRTY RED
Chicken hawk came in my yard.

BING
Nah, nah, I'm the one who did it.

TUCKER
Anybody is going down it should be me.

(REVERNED JAMESON enters.)

REVERNED JAMESON
Y'all will sing a different tune before this day is over with. Just mark my word.

CANDY
Reverend Jameson, why are you here? Go on home.

REVERNED JAMESON
(to Candy)
This is my place, Candy. I ain't got no home if they burn this place down.

REVERNED JAMESON (CONT'D)
Can't y'all understand what I'm trying to say to y'all?

(Nobody says anything.)

REVERNED JAMESON
(to Mathu)
Mathu, for God's sake, please turn yourself in. Please Mathu.

(MATHU says nothing.)

REVERNED JAMESON
(to Clatoo)
Clatoo, please, talk to him. You got some sense. Tell him what can happen.

CLATOO
I come here to stand, not to talk.

REVERNED JAMESON
That's what y'all came here for? To die? Y'all think that'll make up for all the hurt. That's what y'all think?

CANDY
Go home, Jameson. I don't have to tell you anymore.

REVERNED JAMESON
Go home? Go home? Why don't you tell all these old fools to go home? Go home, Old fools, Go home.

CLATOO
Reverend Jameson, nobody listening to you. Just go on home like Candy said.

MAT
You old boot licker, shut up! And get out of here.

REVERNED JAMESON
Whatchu say to me?

MAT
Come on! What?! Whatcha gonna do.

(REVERNED JAMESON and MAT come at face to face yelling at each other. MEN trying to block from MAT and REVERNED JAMESON fighting.)

REVERNED JAMESON
Are you out of your mind? Do you know who you talkin to?

MAT
Yeah, I have lost my mind.

REVERNED JAMESON
You are gonna lose your life you won't be around your wife.

MAT
I don't give a damn. I DON'T GIVE A DAMN. I will shoot you too.

(All the men push REVERNED JAMESON away from MAT. His Bible drops on the ground.)

REVERNED JAMESON

Are you satisfied, Candy? Are you all satisfied? You think you doing him any good if you soak this land with blood? Y'all think y'all can fool Mapes? This man laying here dead on Mathu's yard, the tractor still running, right in front of Mathu's house. Y'all live ten, twelve miles from here. Y'all all gone plumb crazy?

CANDY

JAMESON GET OUT OF HERE AND GO ON HOME.

MAT

Maybe I ought you to shoot him. Should I, Clatoo?

CLATOO

No, Mat.

CLATOO

Reverend, just go on home. Nobody listening to you. Just go.

REVERNED JAMESON

Humph.

(REVERNED JAMESON picks up his bible from the ground and takes his leave. LOU enters.)

LOU

Hey, Reverend Jameson. What's going on here?

REVERNED JAMESON

You better ask her, Mr. Lou. Candy done told me to shut up and go home.

(REVERNED JAMESON exit.)

CANDY

(to Clatoo)

Did Everybody shoot?

CLATOO

(showing her a shoe box filled shells)

We shot. We kept the empty shells.

CANDY

All number fives?

CLATOO
All number fives.

(CANDY sees LOU and she smiles.)

CANDY
Hey.

LOU
Hi.

(CANDY and LOU embrace each other.)

CANDY
I'm glad you could make it. I shot Beau.

(LOU laughs.)

LOU
Oh yeah, and I shot Martin Luther King and John F. Kennedy.
Looks like we're in the same…. page.

(LOU sees All the Men with their shot guns.)

LOU
Candy, what the hell is going on here?

(LOU sees the dead body. He lifts the sheets to see. He looks away from the body and covers his avoiding the rotten dead aroma.)

MAT
I'm the one.

BING
I did it.

CLATOO
I kilt him.

DIRTY RED
I killed him.

(All the MEN chorus saying "I did it! I shot him!". LOU stares at CANDY.)

LOU
I know you lying, Candy.

CANDY
I ain't lying, Lou.

LOU
Candy, I know you for three years, and I know you didn't shot Beau. And what are they doing here?

CANDY
To protect me, I suppose.

LOU
Since when?

(CANDY says nothing. LOU pulls CANDY aside.)

LOU
(quietly)
You don't think Mathu could've done this. Did he? Did he?

CANDY
Look, I said I did it. I did it!

LOU
No you didn't Candy.

CANDY
Yes, I did!

LOU
No you didn't.

CANDY
Yes, I did! I shot him! I shot him!

LOU
Oh Candy.

(CANDY starts to tear up. LOU and CANDY embrace each other.)

LOU
You called Mapes?

CANDY
Miss Merle was down here. I told her to call him after you went by.

(CANDY wipes her tears.)

LOU
For God's sake, Candy, before Mapes gets here, tell me the truth. Did Mathu do this or not?

CANDY
Look, I've already told the truth. I killed him. I killed that son of a bitch.

LOU
You know Fix is going to demand a negro's blood, Candy.

CANDY
That's what I'm going to tell Mapes, what I'm going to tell radio, and what I'm going to give television. I killed that son of bitch. Now, I called you here because I need you to stand beside me. Because I don't have anybody else. But if you don't want to stay, you can go back to Baton Rouge. I don't beg.

(A sound of Sheriff alarm offstage. SHERIFF MAPES enters. MAPES takes out his handkerchief.)

MAPES
(wipes his forehead)
Woo! Hot out here!

(MAPES sees ALL the MEN with their shotguns.)

MAPES
Afternoon folks.

(MAPES sees the DEAD BODY. He looks under the sheets.)

MAPES
Tsk-tsk.

MAPES (CONT'D)
Griffin! Griffin!

(GRIFFIN enters.)

GRIFFIN
You said something, Sheriff?

MAPES
Turn that thing off.

GRIFFIN
(confused)
Sir?

MAPES
The tractor. Dammit. Turn the tractor off.

GRIFFIN
Oh.

(GRIFFIN exit to turn the tractor off.)

MAPES
Oh! And Griffin.

GRIFFIN (O.S)
Yes sir?

(Tractor turns off. GRIFFIN enters.)

MAPES
Get on that radio. Tell Russ. No one else. Russell to go to the back on that bayou and keep Fix there. No one else but him and keep Fix and that crowd back there until he hears from me. And tell Herman to come out here and pick this up. And don't tell him who it is.

GRIFFIN
Yessir.

(GRIFFIN exit. MAPES starts to count the Men with guns.)

MAPES
(counting)
One, two, three, four, five,…

(MAPES continues to count the MEN in silent. GRIFFIN enters.)

GRIFFIN
He's on his way, sir.

MAPES
Thank you, Griffin.

MAPES
Hmmm. All I counted fourteen. Is that all of them?

MAPES
(to Candy)
And you?

CANDY
I don't know how many there are. But I can tell you what happened. I killed him.

MAPES
Really? Over what?

CANDY
Beau Boutan still lived in the past. He still thought he could beat people like his paw did thirty, forty years ago. He started beating Charlie back there in the field, and Charlie ran up here in Mathu's house. Beau followed him in his tractor with his shotgun. So, I shot him. You just don't threaten someone with a shotgun and hunt them like they're wild animals.

CANDY (CONT'D)
Believe me. I'll swear to it in court.
(points at Lou)
And that's my story to the press.

(LOU takes out his notepad and pen.)

MAPES
Humph. Ok.

MAPES
(to Griffin)
Griffin, bring one of them to me.

GRIFFIN
Which one, Sheriff?

MAPES
The one that can talk.

GRIFFIN
Yessir.

(GRIFFIN tries pick one of the MEN.)

CANDY
I said I did it. Why are you questioning them?

LOU
Candy, please!

CANDY
No, because they're black and helpless, is that why you're picking on them?

MAPES
(to Lou)
Keep her out of my sight.

GRIFFIN
(points at Red)
You!

(DIRTY RED stands up and stands on CENTER STAGE. He stands at attention with his shotgun.)

MAPES
Well, well, well, Red. I'm sure everyone calls you Dirty Red. Is that right?

DIRTY RED
Yessir.

MAPES
Alright Red. Whatchu doing behind those trees?

DIRTY RED
I killed him.

MAPES
I just asked you a question. You're not giving me a simple answer.

DIRTY RED
And I'm answering you, I killed him.

(MAPES slaps DIRTY RED.)

CANDY
Hey!

LOU
(stopping Candy)
Candy, stop!

(LOU pulls CANDY away.)

CANDY
(warning)
I'm gonna remember that, Mapes.

LOU
Be easy with him Mapes. He's an old man.

CANDY
(to Lou)
Is that what you gonna do?

LOU
What else do you want me to do, Candy? I could go to jail. Is that what you want? Me to go to jail?

(CANDY ignores.)

MAPES
(to Griffin)
Griffin, get me another.

GRIFFIN
Yessir.

MAPES
(to Dirty Red)
You, stand over there.

(DIRTY RED stands right where MAPES wants him to stand. GRIFFIN picks BILLY WASHINGTON. BILLY stands up.)

MAPES
Ah! Uncle Billy, come on down.

(BILLY WASHINGTON stands on CENTER STAGE at attention with his gun.)

MAPES
How come you live so far, Uncle Billy?

BILLY WASHINGTON
I kilt him.

(MAPES takes BILLY WASHINGTON'S gun. He takes a whiff of his gun.)

MAPES
Seems castoff.

(MAPES gives BILLY's gun back to him.)

MAPES
You ever seen a man in an electric chair?

BILLY WASHINGTON
No sir.

MAPES
Well, it ain't even a pretty sight seeing a man electrocuted in the electric chair.

MAPES (CONT'D)
Now imagine that man sitting in the electric chair dancing, making faces while he's getting electrocuted is you.

(BILLY WASHINGTON says nothing.)

MAPES
Now, I don't have time, Uncle Billy. This is my fishing season and I expect you, Mat, and Chimley down at the Charles fishing. Now I'm gonna ask you again, how come you live so far?

BILLY WASHINGTON
Cus I kilt him.

(MAPES slaps BILLY WASHINGTON.)

CANDY
Why don't use a hose or a stick?

MAPES
(to Griffin)
Griffin, I said the one that can talk. Didn't I?

GRIFFIN
Yessir.

MAPES
Stand him over there, bring me another one.

GRIFFIN
Yessir.

(GRIFFIN pulls BILLY WASHINGTON aside next to DIRTY RED.)

CANDY
You're going to beat them all, Mapes?

MAPES
And Get her out of here.

CANDY
This is my land, in case you forget.

MAPES
Stay of my way, Candy.

CANDY
Like hell.

MAPES
Like hell you won't.

(GRIFFIN picks GABLE. GABLE stands up and stands CENTER STAGE at attention with his shotgun.)

MAPES
What are doing behind those trees, Gable?

GABLE
I kilt him.

MAPES
Now Gable, come on, I don't want to hurt you. You've had enough trouble in your life already.

GABLE
I shot him.

(MAPES slaps GABLE.)

MAPES
Oh I'm sorry, Gable. Did that hurt?

GABLE
No.

(MAPES slaps GABLE again.)

MAPES
How about now? Feel the pain?

(GABLE nods. MAPES slaps him again.)

CANDY
Mapes, you better cut it out.

MAPES
(to Gable)
Get out of my sight.

MAPES
Bring me another, Griffin.

(GRIFFIN picks YANK. YANK stands up and stands CENTER STAGE at attention with his shotgun.)

MAPES
Alright, Yank.

YANK
Yessir.

MAPES
I hope you're not gonna waste my time.

YANK
I kilt him.

MAPES
You didn't let me ask you a question, Yank. Whatchu doing on Mathu's porch here?

YANK
I did it. I kilt him.

(MAPES slaps YANK.)

YANK
I could do that all day long.

(MAPES raise his hand to slap.)

CANDY
(block)
I'm next, Mapes.

CANDY (CONT'D)
Hit me Mapes. What are you waiting for?

(All MEN except MATHU stand in a line behind CANDY.)

CLATOO
We ready for you, Mapes.

(MAPES looks at LOU. LOU takes out his cigarette. MAPES walks toward to LOU.)

LOU
(handing Mapes a cigarette)
Smokes, Sheriff?

MAPES
No thanks, I quit.

LOU
Since when, Sheriff.

(LOU lights his cigarette and smokes.)

MAPES
Ever since Ida passed on.

LOU
Oh. Hmm.

LOU (CONT'D)
Sorry about her.

MAPES
Yeah thanks.

(MAPES stares at MATHU.)

MAPES
You know he did it, don't you?

LOU
Who?

MAPES
You know who I'm talking about?

(LOU stares at MATHU.)

LOU
Why don't you arrest him?

MAPES
On what charges?

LOU
Killing Beau, I suppose.

MAPES
How can I prove it? Because Beau was killed here in the yard? That's no proof. Clinton would have that thrown out of court in two seconds flat. And she knows that too.

LOU
What about the gun?

MAPES
They all have twelve-gauge shotguns. Everyone probably has the same numbered shell in the gun right now. No, you can't arrest him on that. But he killed him, all right. The only one with nuts enough to do it.

(MAPES reaches into his pocket, pulls out a mint Lifesaver, and puts it in his mouth.)

MAPES
You seen Charlie?

LOU

No, I haven't seen him.

MAPES

He's probably hiding somewhere back there in the field. We pick him up anytime. But he didn't do it. And she arranged this little get-together. Not him. He never would have. He's a tough old goat just like you see him there. He probably would have turned himself in by now if she hadn't got into it, but he doesn't want to go against her. Where she got all old men from, only God knows. Look at them. Look at those old guns.

MAPES (CONT'D)

My God, can't you talk to her? I don't want any trouble on this place. That Baton Rouge crowd's already getting drunk for that game tomorrow. Some of them wouldn't want anything better than a necktie party tonight.

LOU

I tried talking. She wouldn't listen.

MAPES

You tried throwing her ass into the back of the car?

LOU

No I didn't try that, Mapes. I hear there's a law against kidnapping people. Especially on their own place.

MAPES

There's a law against harboring a murderer, too. You ever heard of that law?

(LOU says nothing.)

MAPES

Well, you two will make a hell of a marriage.

LOU

Don't get personal, Mapes.

MAPES

When is the date?

LOU

Just don't get personal, Mapes, all right?

(MAPES chuckles. LOU drops his cigarette on the ground and stomps on it.)

MAPES

Maybe Beau was living in the past, and maybe he wasn't, but she damned sure is. She still thinks she can do as her paw and the rest of them did fifty years ago. Well, it's not going to work. He isn't getting out of this.

LOU

You seem to have something personal against him.

MAPES

That's where you're wrong. I admire that man. He's better man than most I've met, black or white. But he killed a man, and she's not getting him out of it. If she had any sense at all, she would have taken him to jail hours ago. Because if Fix doesn't show up, others may. And they won't be coming here to talk. But I don't suppose she realizes that.

(A sound of a CAR approaching at MATHU's house.)

MAPES

Well here comes Herman.

(MAPES sees CANDY and the MEN still line up.)

MAPES

(to Men and Candy)

Y'all still gonna stand on a line, all day?

CANDY

Pretty much, Mapes.

(HERMAN, the coroner enters.)

MAPES

Herman, good to see you.

HERMAN

Mapes.

(HERMAN looks around. He sees the DEAD BODY.)

MAPES

Don't you think you ought to get started?

HERMAN

Sure, Mapes.

(HERMAN glances and examines at the DEAD BODY.)

MAPES

How long you reckon he's been dead?

HERMAN
Two, maybe three hours I suppose.

MAPES
More like three. That would put it around noon, wouldn't it?

HERMAN
Around the time, I suppose.

MAPES
(to self)
I been here half an hour. Got here around two-thirty. That would have given them-her-a two-and-a half-hour jump-

HERMAN
What?

MAPES
Nothing. Just talking to myself.

HERMAN
I need someone to get the stretcher and blanket.

MAPES
Griffin, go get the stretcher and the blanket.

GRIFFIN
Yessir.

(GRIFFIN exit.)

HERMAN
What the hell is going on here, Mapes? Care to explain. All these old black men with shotguns, a white man laying here dead, and you standing here.

MAPES
You take care of your business, I'll take care of mine.

(GRIFFIN enters with a stretcher and a blanket.)

MAPES
(to Griffin)
Help him out!

(GRIFFIN pulls the stretcher next to HERMAN, and slowly puts it down.)

GRIFFIN
Where do you want me to grab?

HERMAN
Grab his head, I'll grab his legs.

GRIFFIN
Ok.

HERMAN
No wait! You grab his legs, I'll take his head.

HERMAN (CONT'D)
No wai-

MAPES
Could y'all please grab something? Stop wasting time.

GRIFFIN
I'll grab his legs.

HERMAN
Alright.

(GRIFFIN grabs the DEAD BODY legs and HERMAN grabs the top of DEAD BODY.)

HERMAN
Keep the sheet on him. Cover him up with the blanket.

(GRIFFIN covers the DEAD BODY. He trips. Some MEN laugh. GRIFFIN gets up.)

MAPES
Whatcha y'all laughing at?

(MEN stop laughing. GRIFFIN moves the stretcher to the exit.)

MAPES
Herman?

HERMAN
Huh?

MAPES
Don't spread this around.

HERMAN
Oh no, Mapes. I won't tell a soul. I'll just tell them Beau has a chill in all this hot weather that's why I got him all covered up.

MAPES
The rest of it, I mean.

HERMAN
The shotguns?

MAPES
Exactly.

HERMAN
Don't worry, Mapes. I won't tell a soul. Besides, nobody would believe me anyhow. Would you?

(MAPES says nothing. GRIFFIN enters. HERMAN exit. A sound of CAR driving away.)

MAPES
All right. The ones don't stay here get moving.

(Nobody moved.)

MAPES
What's the matter with you all? Can't y'all hear? I said move.

BILLY WASHINGTON
I kilt him.

(MAPES stares at BILLY WASHINGTON.)

MAPES
Billy?

BILLY WASHINGTON
Yessir.

MAPES
Come over here. Everybody get on the porch.

(All the MEN scatter from the line and sit on the porch. CANDY follows BILLY WASHINGTON, but LOU pulls her away from BILLY WASHINGTON.)

MAPES
You still go to church, Uncle Billy?

BILLY WASHINGTON
A deacon at Little Shadrack Baptist Church.

MAPES
You read your Bible, Uncle Billy?

BILLY WASHINGTON
Yessir.

MAPES
If I got a Bible in my hand, would you still say you shot Beau, Uncle Billy?

BILLY WASHINGTON
Well?

MAPES
You didn't shot Beau, now, did you, Uncle Billy?

BILLY WASHINGTON
Yessir, Sheriff. I did it.

MAPES
Candy, put you up to this, no, didn't she? Don't worry, I won't let her do you anything. I promise you.

BILLY WASHINGTON
No sir, I did it all on my own.

MAPES
Was Candy down here when you got here?

BILLY WASHINGTON
I don't rightly know.

MAPES
What do you mean you don't rightly know? That's her car out there. Was her car here?

BILLY WASHINGTON
I can't rightly tell.

MAPES
You mean you can't rightly see?

BILLY WASHINGTON
Oh, I can see well, Sheriff, pretty well indeed.

MAPES
When did you hear about the killing? One o'clock?

BILLY WASHINGTON
I didn't hear about it. I was right here, and I shot him.

MAPES
You think you too old to die in the chair?

BILLY WASHINGTON
No sir.

MAPES
Well, you know what, you're this close getting electrocuted, Uncle Billy. You know that?

BILLY WASHINGTON
Yessir I know.

MAPES
(annoyed)
I don't have all day, Uncle Billy.

BILLY WASHINGTON
I kilt him.

MAPES
Then why?

BILLY WASHINGTON
Sir?

MAPES
Then, why did you kill Beau?

BILLY WASHINGTON
Beau beat my boy. He beat him down til they beat him crazy, and we had to send him to Jackson. He don't even know me and his mama no more.

MAPES
When did this happen, Uncle Billy?

BILLY WASHINGTON
Years back, when he came back from the war.

MAPES
What war?

BILLY WASHINGTON
That war with Hitler and them Japs.

MAPES
You've been holding a grudge against Fix all time, Uncle Billy?

BILLY WASHINGTON
I don't hold no grudge. My Bible tells me not to hold no grudge.

MAPES
Well does your Bible says thou shalt not kill?

BILLY WASHINGTON
Yes it does.

MAPES

Even though the Bible, it says, “thou shalt not kill”. Then why did you kill Beau?

BILLY WASHINGTON

Sometimes you just must go against your Bible, Sheriff. And like I said, he beat my boy up, so I shot him.

MAPES

Get out of my sight, Uncle Billy.

BILLY WASHINGTON

Yessir, I’m moving. But I did it.

MAPES

I told you to move.

(BILLY WASHINGTON moves away from MAPES. BLACKOUT. END OF SCENE EIGHT.)

ACT ONE

SCENE NINE

SETTING: Fix's House; Backyard

AT RISE: FIX BOUTAN is painting his new fence outside of his house. A sound of CAR approaching.

RUSSELL (O.S)
Fix? Fix?

FIX
Over here.

(SHERIFF RUSSELL enters.)

FIX
Hey, Sheriff Russell, what brings you here? I hope there's no bad news.

RUSSELL
I'm afraid there is, and I guarantee you you're not gonna like this news. Your son Beau is dead.

FIX
(stops painting)
What? How?

RUSSELL
Your son Beau was found dead outside of a black man's home. Sheriff Mapes is down there at the quarters, he's not giving any details on what happen.

FIX
Tell me Mapes didn't just find my son laying there dead. Don't tell me he was killed by a nigger. Was he?

RUSSELL
I believe so.

FIX
Oh my God! My dear boy! My son!

(FIX puts his paintbrush down.)

FIX
(calling out)
A-goose, Get the family together. Some nigger killed my son.

(FIX BOUTAN picks up his tools and exit. BLACKOUT. END OF SCENE NINE.)

ACT ONE

SCENE TEN

SETTING: Louisiana State University; Football Field

AT RISE: SULLY, GIL BOUTAN, and CAL HARRISON, three LSU football teammates, playing football.

SULLY
(imitating a sportscaster)
Boutan runs right, then he dodges left.

CAL
Salt, I'm open.

(GIL pass the ball to CAL.)

SULLY
He passes the ball to Cal "Pepper" Harrison. And…

(CAL runs and hits a touchdown.)

SULLY, GIL, CAL
Touchdown!

(GIL and CAL chest bump each other.)

SULLY
(imitating a sportscaster)
Oh my goodness! Ladies and Gents the LSU are the new champions. And the Crowd goes wild. AAAH!

(All three men have a laugh and sit on the bench. FOOTBALL ASSISTANT COACH enters.)

ASSISTANT COACH
Gil! Gil!

GIL
Huh?

ASSISTANT COACH
Coach wants to see you.

GIL
Aw man, I thought we had gone all over that.

ASSISTANT COACH
I don't think it's football this time.

SULLY & CAL
Ooh!

GIL
Oh, boy! Alright I'm coming.

SULLY
(mouth to Gil)
What did you do?

GIL
(mouth back)
I don't know.

(GIL gets up and exit with ASSISTANT COACH.)

CAL
(to Sully)
Hey, I wonder what they're talkin about?

SULLY
I don't know. Probably something he did. Or something you both did.

CAL
What do you mean? We didn't do anything. Even if it had something to do with me, Coach would've call me and Gil to the office.
I'm sure whatever it is. I'm sure Coach is gonna give him a warning.

SULLY
Yeah cus we need Gil. We can't play at the Sugar Bowl without him.

CAL
Right.

(GIL now upset enters. SULLY and CAL see GIL upset.)

SULLY
Gil, what happened?

CAL
Salt, what's the matter?

GIL
My brother, he got killed.

CAL
in a wreck?

GIL
No.

(GIL starts to cry.)

GIL
(in tears)
Why today?

(CAL place his on GIL'S shoulder.)

SULLY
Gil, take it easy.

CAL
Yeah man. It's gonna be okay.

(GIL makes an angry face at CAL, moves CAL's hand away from his shoulder and walks away.)

CAL
(stunned)
Salt?!

SULLY
Gil, that's Cal. That's Pepper, man. Gil?

GIL
Why today, Sully? Why?

SULLY
It's okay, Gil. It's gonna be okay.

GIL
I have to get home. Can I borrow your car? Mines still in the shop.

(SULLY reaches into his pockets and pulls out his car keys.)

SULLY
(hands Gil the keys)
Here.

GIL
Thanks. I'll give your car back. I promise.

SULLY
Ok. Take it easy, Gil.

(GIL exit. BLACKOUT. END OF SCENE TEN.)

ACT ONE

SCENE ELEVEN

SETTING: Outside of Mathu's house

AT RISE: Its near evening. GRIFFIN is taking a cigarette break, SHERIFF MAPES is sitting on a chair reading a newspaper. Everybody else sitting on the porch including CANDY sitting next to CLATOO.

CANDY
Clatoo?

CLATOO
Hmmm.

CANDY
You know why, don't you, Clatoo?

(CLATOO put his arm around CANDY.)

CLATOO
I know why, Candy. I know he looked out for you all your life. You'd do anything in the world, wouldn't you?

(CANDY nods. MAPES stares at MATHU.)

MAPES
Mathu? Come here.

(MATHU stands up with his gun.)

CANDY
Stay where you at.

MATHU
I'll come to the man.

(MATHU comes toward MAPES. CANDY follows.)

CANDY
(to Mapes)
Hey Mapes. Mind your hands. He ain't no Yank, Red, Gable, or Billy. But Mind your hands now.

(CANDY sits back at the porch.)

MAPES
How you feeling, Mathu?

MATHU
Fine, Sheriff. You?

MAPES
Tired. I had thought I'd get a little fishing in today.

MATHU
They biting good, what I hear.

MAPES
Tell them to go home, Mathu.

MATHU
That's up to them, Sheriff.

MAPES
They'll do it if you tell them to do it. Tell them to go home before there's trouble.

CANDY
Mathu, you don't have to answer any questions.

MATHU
I don't mind talking to the man, Candy.

(CANDY stays silent.)

MAPES
Tell them to tell me who did it, Mathu.

MATHU
I did it, Sheriff.

MAPES
I know you did it. You're the only one around here man enough. But I must hear it from one of them. One of them must say he was called here after it happened.

MATHU
I can't make nobody say what they don't want to say.

MAPES
Do you want to see any of these people hurt, Mathu?

MATHU
No Sheriff.

MAPES
You know that can happen now, don't you?

MATHU

A man got to do what he thinks is right, Sheriff. That's what part of him from a boy.

MAPES

It's not a matter of right and wrong, Mathu. It's a matter of a lot of people getting hurt. And you know you don't want that.

MATHU

No sir. I don't. But it's up to them.

MAPES

It's up to you, Mathu. Only you. And I ask you, man to man, tell them to go home.

CLATOO

It ain't go'n work this time, Sheriff.

MAPES

Who said that?

(CLATOO stands up.)

CLATOO

I did Sheriff.

MAPES

Clatoo, what's the matter with you? You're the last person I thought would be looking for trouble.

CLATOO

That's been my trouble.

MAPES

What?

(MAPES comes toward CLATOO.)

CLATOO

I ain't had no trouble with the law.

MAPES

Meaning?

CLATOO

I'm old.

MAPES

Meaning?

CLATOO
About time I had a lil trouble with the law before I die.

MAPES
You really want to go to jail, don't you?

CLATOO
I figured I was on my way there when I shot him.

JACOB
Amen.

MAPES
Isn't it a little bit late for you to be getting militant around here?

CLATOO
I always been militant. My intrance gone sour, keeping my militance down.

MAPES
Sure now.

CLATOO
Sure now is right. No use talking to Mathu. He didn't do nothing. I did it.

DIRTY RED
Now, there y'all go again, there y'all go again. I don't see how come y'all won't let a man get-

MAPES
Red, shut up! You and nobody in your family ever done a thing in this in this world but worked hard to avoid work.

DIRTY RED
Till today. Today I-

MAPES
You trying to cut in on me when I'm talking to you?

JOHNNY PAUL
Looks like he's doing more than just trying.

MAPES
You too, Johnny Paul? You want to go down with him?

JOHNNY PAUL
Yeah, me too and I don't mind going.

JACOB

No, Dirty Red, Johnny Paul. Uh-uh, Clatoo. It was me. I remember what that crowd did to my sister.

MAPES

I see.

JACOB

You see what? You don't see, Sheriff.

DING

I kilt him. Me, not them. Me, I did it. What they did to my sisters' little girl, Michelle Gigi.

MAPES

I see.

DING

You don't see nothing, Sheriff. All you can see is them weeds right here.

JOHNNY PAUL

Y'all remember how it used be? When they wasn't no weeds, remember? Remember how they used to sit out there on the garry. Mama, Aunt Clara, Aunt Sarah, Unc Moon, Aunt Spoodle, Aunt Thread. Remember? Everybody had flowers in the yard. But nobody had four-o'clocks like Jack Toussaint. Every day at four o'clock, they opened up just as pretty, Remember? Rufe, you worked at Jack garry before, Remember? That's why I killed him, that's why. To protect them little flowers. But they ain't here no more. How come?

GABLE

Remember Jack and Red Rider hitting that field every morning with them mules, Diamond and Job?

(Nobody says anything.)

GABLE

Lord, don't tell me you can't remember them early mornings when that sun was just coming up over there behind them trees. Jack and Red Rider used to race out into that field on them old single slides. Jack with Diamond, Red Rider with Job touching the ground to keep them slides steady. Tell me who could beat them two men plowing a row, hanh? Who?

MAT

Nobody. Them was men.

JOHNNY PAUL

Thirty, forty of us going out in with cane knives, hoes, plows, you name it. Sunup to Sundown, hard, miserable, work but managed to get it done. We stuck together, shared what little we had, loved and respected each other. But just look at things today. Where the people? Where the roses? Where the four-o'clocks? The palm of Christians? Where the people use to sing and pray in the church? I'll tell you. Under the trees back there, that's where. And where they used to stay, the weeds got it now, just waiting for the tractor to come plow it up.

GABLE

There's something you can't see, Sheriff. You can't see nothing. You can't see Red Rider with Job, Jack with Diamond. You can't hear them people singing and praying in church. You had to be here to see.

CLATOO

Remember my brother Silas, I know y'all remember Silas, don't y'all? I'm talking to the old, not to the young. You don't remember him, Candy. They got rid of him 'fore you were born. He was the last black man round here trying to sharecrop on this place. The last one to fight against that tractor out there.

TUCKER

We told him to stop. We all told him. We tried to show him it couldn't work. We had got the worst land from the start and no matter how hard we worked on it. After the plantation was dying out, the Marshalls dosed out the land, giving us the worst.

(MAPES grunts.)

TUCKER

Grunt all you want, Sheriff but I'm stating facts. Cause this is the day of reckoning, and I will speak the truth, without fear, if it means I have to spend the rest of my life in jail. If you want to lock me up, go ahead and do it. I'm ready.

GRIFFIN

I wish I was the sheriff around here. I bet they wouldn't be talking to me like that.

MAT

And what would do, you little no-butt nothing?

MAPES
Griffin, shut up!

GRIFFIN
I ain't used to no negros talking to me like that.

CLATOO
Then stick around son.

GRIFFIN
Sheriff, are we gon' stand around here all day and take this?

MAPES
If you don't like it, then take a walk.

GRIFFIN
I don't like walking.

MAPES
Then stand over there and be quiet.

(GRIFFIN stands where MAPES wants him to stand.)

CLATOO
How can a man beat a machine? No way? Hanh? That's what you say? Well, my brother did. With them two little mules, he beat that tractor to the derrick. Them two little mules did all they could, like my brother did. They knowed it was end if they couldn't make it. They had to pull even if they wanted to keep going. They pulled him for sweating, slipping, falling, but pulling for him. And yes, they won. So, they beat him. They took stalks of cane and they beat him and beat him and beat him down. I was there. I don't know how come I am still alive.

(CLATOO tears up.)

CLATOO
(teary)
Silas, my brother, Forgive me! Silas, can you hear me? Forgive me! Where was the law? Where was the law then? How can a man on a wagon made of flesh and blood cut in on a tractor? No way! Ain't no way.... In my fear, even after I had seen what happened. I went along with the white folks. Out of fear of a little pain to my own body, I beat my own brother with a stalk of cane as much as the white folks did.

(A sound of CAR approaches at the quarters. A sound of someone eject out of the CAR. GIL slowly enters.)

JACOB
Who's that?

MAT
That's Gil. Fix's youngest boy.

JACOB
Oh.

(MAPES comes towards GIL.)

MAPES
Gil.

(GIL glances at all the MEN with shotguns. He sees the area where his brother BEAU was found dead.)

GIL
Where is my brother, Mapes?

MAPES
They took him into Bayonne. I got Russell back there on the bayou. I told him to keep your daddy back there. I don't want him here at Marshall, Gil. I don't want him in Bayonne till I send for him. You're on your way home?

(GIL says nothing.)

MAPES
I'll have it over with before sundown.

GIL
What over with, Mapes?

MAPES
The person who did it. I'll have him in jail before you know it. I guarantee that.

GIL
Don't you know who did it?

MAPES
I think I do. I'm sure I do.

GIL
Then why don't you arrest him?

MAPES
They all say they did it.

GIL
But you know who did it?

MAPES
Yes, I know who did it.

GIL
Your way? How long my brothers been dead? Four hours?

(GIL stares at MATHU.)

GIL
(to Mathu)
You, Mathu?

MATHU
Yes.

GIL
You know what happened to my brother.

MATHU
Yes, I did it. I killed him.

(GIL looks at MAPES.)

GIL
(to Mapes)
Mapes, what the hell is going on here?

(MAPES takes a Mint Lifesaver out of his pocket.)

MAPES
Ask them. Or better yet ask Candy.

(MAPES puts a Mint Lifesaver in his mouth. GIL stares at CANDY. CANDY tries not to looks at GIL.)

GIL
What is going on here, Candy?

CANDY
Beau tried to chase Big Charlie with a shot gun.

GIL
LIAR! You're lying, Candy. My brother would never come after Charlie with a gun. A stick, A stalk of cane, but never with a gun. Why are you here in the first place?

(CANDY ignores GIL. GIL turns to LOU.)

GIL
What's going on here, Lou?

LOU
I don't know. She wouldn't say.

GIL
Lou, I know you. You must know something. Tell me.

LOU
Gil, believe me. I don't know anything.

(GIL sees a lone shotgun laying and grabs the shotgun. GIL furiously holds and stare at the shotgun.)

GIL
(throws shotgun to ground)
WHEN IS THIS EVER GONNA STOP? HUH? WON'T IT EVER STOP?

MAPES
Gil, come on.

GIL
(furious)
Let go of me, Sheriff.

GIL
(to Men)
Won't it ever stop?

(The MEN say nothing. CANDY looks away from GIL, not saying a single word.)

GIL
(to Candy)
You did this, Candy. You never did like Beau. Hell, you never liked any of us. If only you knew how sad, how pathetic you look. You're pathetic.

(CANDY says nothing.)

MAPES
Come on, Gil.

(GIL stares at the area where his brother BEAU was killed at. He comes toward at the spot. He kneels and does "the Father, the Son, the Holy Spirit" prayer gesture in front the spot.)

GIL
(teary eyed)
I do all I can to stop it. Won't it ever stop?

(GIL furiously stares at everyone and then exits. MAPES follows GIL.)

LOU
Candy, come on. Don't you think it is high time for you to leave these men alone?

CANDY
I'm not leaving. This is my land, I ain't going nowhere, Lou.

(LIGHTS DIM TO BLACKOUT. END OF ACT ONE.)

ACT II

SETTING:

Louisiana

TIME:

1970s

ACT TWO

SCENE ONE

SETTING: Outside of Mathu's House

AT RISE: The next day, after the murder of BEAU BOUTAN. It's the afternoon. SHERIFF MAPES is snoozing on the chair with a newspaper laying his chest. CLATOO is playing chess with TUCKER, YANK plays the violin, DIRTY RED is cracking nuts with his gun and sharing it with the MEN, Some Men are sitting having a conversation and MATHU is tending his garden. SNOOKUM is playing football with LOU. CANDY enters from MATHU'S house dressed in a casual outfit. LOU stops playing with SNOOKUM and hands him his football back.

LOU
(smiles)
Hey.

CANDY
(smiles back)
Hey.

(They kiss. He holds her close.)

CANDY
Did you find spiders over there?

LOU
No. Just cobwebs.

CANDY
Hmmm.

LOU
Listen, why don't you do yourself a favor?

CANDY
What?

LOU
You go home, take a shower and get some rest. I'll stay here and give you a heads up.

CANDY
No, I don't want to. I'm not leaving without Mathu. Besides, they're my people.

LOU
Candy, you haven't slept, and you barely ate. Come on, at least go for-.

CANDY
Lou, I love you and all, but like I told you and Mapes this before already. I ain't going nowhere. Ok?

LOU
If you say so.

CANDY
I'm going to go freshen up. Ok?

LOU
Ok. You do that.

CANDY
Keep an eye on Mathu for me. Don't stand there and look at me. Go!

(CANDY exit. LOU is upset, he sits on the porch with MATHU.)

LOU
I'll never get the chance or time with her, Will I? She only cares for you.

MATHU
Me? Why me?

LOU
Because she's always protective of you. Mathu this and Mathu that. I'm trying to start a life with her. What about me?

MATHU
Why does she needs to protect me? She's a grown woman she needs to protect herself not me. I don't need no protection.

MATHU (CONT'D)
Look, I like you, Lou. You seemed like a nice boy. Know how to treat a woman right. Can't think what man would ever be with Candy. Even Candy, I know she's crazy about you. She'll turn around. Give her some time. Maybe today or maybe tomorrow.

LOU
No, she won't.

LOU (CONT'D)
I work so hard, Mathu. Doing everything I can for her. I work hours every day saving up money for her, to build our future together, buy a nice big house, and start a family.

MATHU
You saying you want to marry her?

LOU
Now you starting to talk like Mapes.

MATHU
You want to marry her?

LOU
Well…Of course, I do. I love her. I've been with for years.

MATHU
What are waiting for?

(MISS MERLE carrying a lunch basket enters.)

MISS MERLE
(waking up Mapes)
Mapes?

(MAPES snorts loud.)

MISS MERLE
Mapes? Mapes?

MAPES
(waking up)
Huh? What!?!

MISS MERLE
Wake up.

MAPES
(yawn)
Miss Merle, what time is it?

MISS MERLE
It's noon.

MAPES
(looking at his wristwatch)
Oh.

MISS MERLE
I bought sandwiches and more food is in the trunk.

(MAPES sees MISS MERLE'S sandwich basket. He digs his hand in the basket, takes a sandwich and takes a bite.)

MISS MERLE
I hope you like ham and cheese.

MAPES
(eating his sandwich)
Mmmm. It's good. Did you bring beer?

MISS MERLE
No, Mapes.

MAPES
Hmm. You could've brought beer.

(MISS MERLE rolls her eyes.)

MAPES
Or water would be nice.

MATHU
Snookum! Snookum! Come here.

(SNOOKUM comes toward MATHU.)

MATHU
Go get me that jug of ice water out of the icebox and bring them jelly glasses out of the safe.

SNOOKUM
Ok.

(SNOOKUM exit in MATHU'S house.)

MISS MERLE
(to Everybody)
Excuse me, gentlemen. I brought for food. I made sandwiches.
(to Griffin)
Griffin, would you be a dear and get the rest in the trunk.

GRIFFIN
Sure thing, Miss.

(MISS MERLE gives GRIFFIN the keys to her trunk. GRIFFIN exit. MISS MERLE gives the basket to DING. DING takes a sandwich and passes the basket to the MEN.)

MISS MERLE

Everybody take one sandwich and pass it around.

(GRIFFIN enters with a basket of fried chicken and a silver pot of gumbo. SNOOKUM enters with a jar glass of water.)

MISS MERLE

There is no dessert. There's not enough pie for all of you.

(to Griffin)

Griffin, make sure everyone gets one piece of chicken and one bowl of gumbo.

(SNOOKUM hands the water to MAPES. GRIFFIN exit to get the paper bowls and plastic silverware.)

MAPES

(takes the water)

Thank you.

(MAPES takes a sip.)

MAPES

(to Mathu)

It's too late to go fishing anyhow.

MATHU

Yup.

(LOU sees MISS MERLE.)

LOU

Hey Miss Merle.

MISS MERLE

Oh, Lou, it's good to see you.

(CANDY enters with a towel around her neck. MISS MERLE sees CANDY.)

MISS MERLE

Hey Candy.

CANDY

Hi, Miss Merle.

MISS MERLE

I thought I find you here. Janey told me you would be here.

CANDY

Well you found me.

MISS MERLE
Are you hungry, sweetheart? I made sandwiches for everybody. Also, I bought some chicken and-

CANDY
No thanks, Miss Merle.

MISS MERLE
Candy, you got eat something.

(CANDY takes the sandwich without looking at MISS MERLE.)

CANDY
Thanks, Miss Merle.

MISS MERLE
You're welcome, dear.

(CANDY takes a bite of the sandwich.)

MISS MERLE
(to herself)
Jesus, you ever seen anything like this?

MISS MERLE
(to Candy)
I saw Gil the other day. Poor child. Hmmm.

CANDY
Yeah, well, he can get over it himself.

MISS MERLE
Now Candy!

CANDY
What?

MISS MERLE
Are you satisfied with you and your army?

(CANDY stays silent and continues to eat her sandwich.)

MISS MERLE
Candy?

(CANDY looks at MISS MERLE.)

MISS MERLE
Aren't you listening? When will this ever end? When will this charade?

(SNOOKUM taps MISS MERLE.)

MISS MERLE
What is it, Snookum?

SNOOKUM
Can I have a another?

MISS MERLE
What?

SNOOKUM
Sammich. Candy didn't pay me enough-

(SNOOKUM glance at MAPES. MAPES stares at SNOOKUM.)

MISS MERLE
(gives Snookum a sandwich)
Here.

MAPES
Lou can stand another one, too.

MISS MERLE
You know what?

(MISS MERLE comes toward MAPES.)

MISS MERLE
(hands sandwich to Mapes)
Here. Take it!

MISS MERLE
Now tell me, how long is this charade going on?

MAPES
They all claim they did it? Who should I take in?
(pointing at Candy)
Her?

MISS MERLE
And you're supposed to be a man?

MISS MERLE (CONT'D)
(to Mapes)
Look, Mapes. Tell her to get her butt up the quarters.

MAPES
(chewing sandwich)
Up to her.

MISS MERLE
Since when?

(MAPES continues eating his sandwich, not saying a word to MISS MERLE.)

MISS MERLE
(disappointed)
Let me get away from here.
(to Griffin)
Griffin?

(GRIFFIN comes toward MISS MERLE.)

GRIFFIN
Yes, Miss?

MISS MERLE
Did you serve everyone?

GRIFFIN
Yes Miss.

MISS MERLE
What about Mathu? Did you save his?

GRIFFIN
Yes Miss.

MISS MERLE
Ok. I'm leaving.

(MISS MERLE grabs her stuff.)

MAPES
(stops Miss Merle)
Hold it, Miss Merle.

MISS MERLE
What is it, Mapes?

MAPES
Just want to say thanks for the sandwiches.

(MISS MERLE ignores and then exit. A sound of CAR leaving. MAPES stares at MATHU.)

MAPES
How come you're not eating?

MATHU

Thought I do this before I take my last meal.

MAPES

Hmmm.

(MAPES stares MATHU tending his garden. He comes toward MATHU.)

MAPES

How come you not eating?

MATHU

Thought I do this before I eat.

MAPES

Hey Mathu. Remember that alligator we caught in '53 down at the river.

MATHU

Yeah, I remember Sheriff.

(MATHU smirks a little.)

MAPES

(chuckles)

Yeah.

MAPES (CONT'D)

Mathu, why are you doing this? You know you don't have to do this. I know Candy is the one who set this whole thing. But you don't have to listen to her. You're a man, right? I've always been fair to you. And you know that.

(DIRTY RED stops eating and hears the conversation between MATHU and MAPES.)

MAPES

Just tell them to go home and come with me to the station. That way no one can get hurt. And Everyone will be safe.

DIRTY RED

Sheriff?

MAPES

What is it Red?

DIRTY RED

When has it ever been safe? Hanh? It never been safe for us.

MAPES
Look, Red—

DIRTY RED
Nah Sheriff. We ain't never been safe. Here in Marshall we were never saved. No one tends to look our way. People like you and all the other white folks, y'all look at us like we're nothing but wild animals. You think Beau would ever leave us alone if he was alive and breathin' today. Nah Sheriff you don't see or think. That's why I kilt that bastard so we can keep Marshall safe away from him and the Boutan's.

MAPES
(exhausted)
Oh my God! Are you finish?

DIRTY RED
No I ain't. We ain't run out of stories. We still got more.

MAPES
Enough. I don't want to hear anymore.

MAPES (CONT'D)
So it's all on Fix, hanh? Far as I'm concern y'all run out of stories. Whether he did or didn't do anything. Fix is gonna pay for everything that ever happen to you, huh? Fix didn't change things around here. Progress did.
(to Mat)
And Fix wasn't even there the night Oliver died in the hospital, Mat. You're blaming the wrong man. And you're talking about 30, 40 years ago with no proof that Fix wasn't even any of it.

MAT
We get beaten, lynched, hearing our sisters and our daughters getting raped by the white men or the Boutan's, guts all hanging out. And here he come with ain't no proof who did it. Ain't it just like white folks?

(All MEN agree with MAT.)

MAT
And it ain't been no 40, 50 years ago right here in them demonstrations somebody was always turning missing. Things ain't nicer than nice right here now.

MAPES
I could take you to jail.

MAT
Then I’m ready to go.

JACOB
Me too!

DIRTY RED
Same here.

CLATOO
I’m ready.

(GRIFFIN enters.)

GRIFFIN
Hey Sheriff! I got a word from Russell. Fix brought the whole crowd together. He said about 25 of them are there. And more and more are coming.

MAPES
Hmmm. The quiet before the hurricane. Fix will be here when he gets them all together.

CLATOO
We’ll be here too, Sheriff. We’ll be here.

MAPES
(chuckles)
Then I guess we’ll be one big happy family.

(CANDY grabs MATHU’S arm.)

CANDY
(to Mathu)
You need to sit down?

CANDY (CONT’D)
He hasn’t been feeling well suffering from dizzy spells.

MAPES
I suffer from dizzy spells, too. Every time when I shoot someone.

(BLACKOUT.END OF SCENE ONE.)

ACT TWO

SCENE TWO

SETTING: Boutan's house

AT RISE: Grieving Boutan families and friends arrived at Boutan household. SHERIFF RUSSELL enters. GIL, in tears, sitting on STAGE LEFT.

RUSSELL
You alright?

GIL
(teary eyed)
Yeah.

(GIL wipes his tears.)

GIL
I'm ok.

RUSSELL
Sorry about your brother, son. Take it easy! Alright.

(RUSSELL pats GIL on the shoulder. GIL stands up and sees his family. Grieving Boutan families and friends give GIL hugs, kisses, and sharing their condolences. FIX is sitting on STAGE RIGHT with including AUGUSTE, CLAUDE, JEAN, ALFONZE, LUKE WILL, little brother TEE BEAU, and other Grieving Men.)

FIX
You know you don't have to be here, son. You could go back to school.

(GIL kisses FIX on the side of his face.)

GIL
No Papa. This family matters to me. I took Sully's car to come here.

(FIX hugs GIL.)

FIX
(embracing)
Oh my Gi-bear.

GIL
I passed by Marshall.

FIX
Well?

GIL
He doesn't want you there, Papa.

FIX
Don't want me there? Who don't want me?

GIL
Sheriff Mapes. Sheriff Mapes don't want me at Marshall or Bayonne until he sends for you.

FIX
But why? Why? My boy is laying in the morgue, shot like a dog, and he don't want me at Bayonne.

AUGUSTE
Mapes is crazy.

LUKE WILL
He's got to be crazy.

FIX
Well, He's still at Marshall?

GIL
Yes, Papa.

FIX
What's he doing at Marshall?

GIL
Talking to people.

FIX
Talking to people about what? He doesn't know who did it?

GIL
He thinks Mathu did it.

(All the Men are stunned including FIX. RUSSELL enters.)

FIX
What? But why would Mathu kill my boy?

GIL
He claimed Beau came into his yard with a gun.

FIX
What for?

GIL
He came after Charlie. He came with a gun.

FIX
And Mathu killed him for that?

GIL
That's what Mapes believes.

LUKE WILL
Ain't we wasting time, Fix?

FIX
Luke Will. You might have been a friend of Beau's. But you not a member of this family, and you don't speak.

LUKE WILL
I was closer than a friend. I was a good friend of Beau. We had beer last night.

FIX
You still don't speak. I speak. My sons speak. I tell you when to speak. That's clear, Luke Will?

(LUKE WILL says nothing.)

GIL
Papa, Can I say something?

FIX
What is it, Gi-bear?

GIL
I went to Marshall.

FIX
I know you said that.

GIL
I saw something over there, Papa. Something, you, I, none of us in this room has ever seen before. A bunch of black old men with shotguns, Papa. Old men, your age, Parrin's age, Monsieur Auguste's age Waiting for you.

FIX
(holding Tee Beau)
Niggers with shotguns waiting for me?

GIL

Fifteen and maybe even more. And Mapes there with a pump gun all waiting for you.

LUKE WILL

Then let's accommodate Mapes and his niggers.

(All the MEN shout with agreement.)

GIL

They're Old Men! Papa, they're Old men. Old men. Cataracts. Hardly any teeth. Arthritic. Old black men, Papa who have been hurt. Tired old black men trying hard to hold their heads.

FIX

What are trying to say, Gi-bear?

GIL

Papa, all my life I have heard what my family have done to others. I hear it today, from the blacks, from the whites. I hear it from the opponents even when we play in another town. Don't tackle me too hard, because they would have to answer to the rest of the Boutan's. It hurts me to hear that, Papa.
(touching his chest)
It hurts me here.

FIX

What's that supposed to mean, Gi-bear?

GIL

I want to be an All-American at LSU, Papa. I have a good chance. Cal and me. The first time ever, black and white, in the Deep South. I can't make it without Cal, Papa. I depend on him. Every time I take that ball, I depend on his block, or his faking somebody out of the way. I depend on him, Papa, every moment I'm on that field.

FIX

What about your brother, Gi-bear?

GIL

What about Beau? I loved my brother, Papa. He was much older than me, Yes, we were close. He taught me everything I know about fishing and hunting, but Beau is dead. Ain't no way he is coming back.

FIX

You through, Gi-bear?

GIL

Papa, I won't go along. You can beat me, but I won't go along.

FIX

(to Alfonze and Auguste)

What do you think of our great All-American there, Alfonze? A-goose?

(ALFONZE and AUGUSTE didn't say nothing. FIX looks at CLAUDE, who's holding a beer in his hand.)

FIX

And you, Claude?

CLAUDE

(not looking at Fix)

Whatever you say, Papa.

(CLAUDE drinks his beer.)

FIX

Jean?

JEAN

Papa we ought to talk.

FIX

Then talk.

JEAN

What will do when we go to Bayonne, Papa? Who will go there?

FIX

You don't want to go to Bayonne?

JEAN

I live in Bayonne, Papa. My butcher shop is in Bayonne. But who else is going?

FIX

I go to see my boy, and your brother.

JEAN

And the rest of these, Papa. Why are they going to Bayonne?

FIX

Your brother was brutally murdered.

JEAN

I know Papa.

FIX
You forget so easily, Jean?

JEAN
No, Papa, I don't forget so easily. But Gilly is right. We have law out there to do what many of these people would like to see us do. Some of these in the room with us right now.

JEAN (CONT'D)
If they're friends of the family, show respect to the family. Stay out of Bayonne until Mapes has cleared this up.

LUKE WILL
Mapes will never clear this up. Beau's been shot down like a dirty dog, and Mapes hasn't done a goddam thing about it.

RUSSELL
Don't y'all listen to Luke Will. All he and that gang want is trouble.

LUKE WILL
What gang's that, Russell?

RUSSELL
You know what gang.

LUKE WILL
Scared to call their names?

RUSSELL
Everybody in here knows who I'm talking about. Don't listen to Luke Will, Fix. He's no friend.

FIX
He's a friend.

LUKE WILL
Give the word, Fix.

FIX
What word is that, Luke Will?

LUKE WILL
We go to Marshall.

FIX
That's my decision to make, Luke Will, and my sons. Not yours.

LUKE WILL
All right, Fix. I'll wait your decision. Then, I'll go to Marshall.

(LUKE WILL gets up. RUSSELL blocks LUKE WILL.)

RUSSELL
(block)
Don't even try it.

FIX
I won't have none of that in my house.
(to Russell)
And you, Russell, I would be quiet if I were you.

RUSSELL
I'll do anything to keep you back here.

FIX
(gets up)
Russell, you can't keep me back here. Only my sons can keep me back here. You remember that.

RUSSELL
Jean and Gilly are right. Luke Will is wrong. Luke Will wants trouble.

FIX
(raise his voice)
In my house, I say what is right and what is wrong.

(AUGUSTE and JEAN try to calm FIX down.)

FIX
(pointing his right hand)
I decide. Me, William Fix Boutan, I decide.

(FIX sits down.)

FIX
(to Alfonze)
What should I do, Alfonze?

ALFONZE
I go whatever you decide, Fix.

FIX
(to Auguste)
A-goose?

AUGUSTE
I'm an old man, Fix. I don't know who is right and who is wrong anymore.

FIX
I'm an old man too. Twenty years ago, I would not have asked questions. I would have been at Marshall by now.

AUGUSTE
I would have been at Marshall with you twenty years ago, Fix.

FIX
They're old as we are. They're waiting for me. According to <u>this</u> All-American here.

AUGUSTE
Old men with guns waiting for old men with guns, Fix, but isn't that a farce?

FIX
And Beau on that cold slab in Bayonne, A-goose? Is that a farce also?

AUGUSTE
I christened him. I'm his parrain. You must know how I feel.

LUKE WILL
Ain't we wasting time, Fix?

FIX
Jean and Gi-bear say no, Luke Will. Even A-goose says no.

LUKE WILL
A-goose is an old man, and don't have sense at all. Gilly and Jean want to keep their good names. All Gilly wants to play football with some niggers.

FIX
(to Gil)
Is that so, Gi-bear? Your brothers honor for the sake to play football with niggers.

GIL
Those days are over, Papa. Luke Will, you know those days are over. This is 70s, soon to be 80s. Those days are gone forever, Papa.

GIL
What day is gone, Gi-bear?

GIL
I'm not speaking on family responsibility. I'm speaking on vigilante.

FIX
So, I'm a vigilante, now?

GIL
That's what Luke Will wants us to do. He and his gang still think the world needs them. The world has changed, Papa.

LUKE WILL
And Beau? He's more alive than I am at this moment?

FIX
Well, Gi-bear?

GIL
Look, Papa. Beau is dead. I'm sorry Papa. But I would like people to know we're not what they think we are. I say let them wait.

FIX
(to Jean)
And you there, Mr. Butcher of hog-gut fame?

JEAN
I go along with Gilly.

FIX
And the rest of you, how you feel? You feel that this, this butcher and this All American got a point.

LUKE WILL
We're wasting time, Fix. Are gonna let them old black gizzards stand there with guns and we don't accommodate them? I say they want war, let's give war.

(A couple of Men shout in agreement.)

FIX
(to Luke Will)
HEY! HEY! Luke Will, I'm not interested in your war, only in my family.

GIL
Papa?

FIX
No, Gi-bear. I have spoken.

FIX
(to Gil)
Now Mr. All American, go on run that football. Let it take the place of family. Let it bring flowers to the cemetery, La Toussaint. I don't wish to see you in the house. Go on, Gi-bear. Leave!

FIX
GET OUT OF MY HOUSE, MR. ALL AMERICAN.

GIL
No, Papa don't send me away. I'm your son. Don't send me away.

(FIX looks away from GIL. Everybody is silent. GIL is stunned and walks away.)

RUSSELL
(stops Gil)
Hey! Hey! Wait!

GIL
What do you think I should do Russ?

RUSSELL
(to Gil)
You know what I think? I think you should do it. Go back to LSU, play that football game tomorrow with Pepper, and play the best damn game you ever play. That's what I think you should do.

GIL
But what about my papa? What's next? Bury him tomorrow?

RUSSELL
What about him? Look son the damage is done. Sometimes you got to hurt something to help something. Sometimes you have to plow under one thing in order for something else to grow. You can help Tee Beau tomorrow. You can help this country tomorrow. You can help yourself.

GIL
(looks away)
Just leave me alone, Russ. Dammit LEAVE ME ALONE!

(GIL exit.)

RUSSELL
Hey, Luke Will Stay away from Marshall.

LUKE WILL
(rolls eyes)
Yeah whatever.

RUSSELL
(serious)
I mean it, Luke Will.

LUKE WILL
No problem, Russ. Me and my boys are just gonna grab a couple drinks at Tee Jack's.

(LUKE WILL and his boys exit. BLACKOUT. END OF SCENE TWO.)

ACT TWO

SCENE THREE

SETTING: Outsides at Mathu's house

AT RISE: It's sunset at Mathu's yard, everyone finished their meals. LOU is sitting with the OLD MEN, interviewing them, taking notes and talking with them. MAPES enters.

MAPES
Alright, Everyone. Looks like you boys put your brave hats just a little too late. Fix ain't coming.

(Everyone is silent until JOHNNY PAUL stands up.)

JOHNNY PAUL
That's a lie.

MAPES
Nope. He's not coming.

MAT
But he's got to come, Sheriff.
(points at the spot)
You see that blood in the grass? That's Fix boy's blood. He's got to show up. He's got to.

JOHNNY PAUL
Just face it, Sheriff. You just want us to leave. You're lying!

MAPES
Why would I lie, Johnny Paul?

MAPES
Now all of y'all pack up and go home.

JOHNNY PAUL
Sheriff, I just called you liar in front of all these men. Aren't you gonna take me in?

MAPES
(to Mathu)
Mathu, you ready?

(Everyone stares at MATHU.)

MATHU
Here I come, Sheriff.

(MATHU stands up. CANDY quickly gets in front of MATHU. CLATOO and MAT follow. The MEN from the porch stand up. They follow as well.)

MAPES
Woah! Hold on! Now I said Mathu.

(The MEN stand still and says nothing.)

MAPES
I said game over. Now go and home.

(All the MEN except MATHU draw the guns at MAPES. GRIFFIN draw his gun at the MEN, some of the MEN draw their shotguns at GRIFFIN.)

CLATOO
Hold it! Hold it! Hold it!

(Everyone lowers their weapons.)

CLATOO
Sheriff, can me and the rest of men talk to Mathu inside?

MAPES
Talk? Talk about what?

CLATOO
Just give us a couple of minutes.

MAPES
All right. I'll give you a couple minutes. Hurry up!

(Half of the Men enter in the house. CANDY follows the Men.)

CLATOO
(stops Candy)
Not you, Candy.

CANDY
Nobody's talking without me.

CLATOO
This time we have to, Candy. Just men with guns.

CANDY
Like hell. This is my place.

CLATOO
I know that, Candy. But this time we don't need you.

CANDY
Who do you think you're talking to? You know where you at? Get the hell off my place.

CLATOO
I'm not going anywhere, Candy.

CANDY
This is my place. This is my land. Y'all can go on listen to Clatoo if y'all want. Remember this, Clatoo got a little piece of land to go back to.

(MAPES starts to laugh. CANDY looks at MAPES.)

MAPES
Well, well, well. Listen to the savior now. Do what she wants or you're out in the cold. That's what you want to keep them as slaves for the rest of their lives.

LOU
Ain't that something.

CANDY
Nobody here is a slave. I'm protecting them. My family has always protected them.

(CANDY stares at MATHU.)

CANDY
(to Mathu)
Mathu, is that what you want?

MATHU
I want you to go home. That's what I want. I'm old. I'm tired, Candy. I got to pay.

(CANDY emotionally hugs MATHU.)

CANDY
(cry)
No, Mathu, no.

MATHU
Go on home, sweetheart. I got to pay.

CANDY
(teary)
No, Mathu, you paid enough. My Daddy and my granddaddy said you paid enough.

MAPES
Griffin, get her off him.

LOU
(stops Griffin)
No, Griffin. I'll do it. Candy will beat you silly.

CANDY
(teary)
This place won't be the same without you.

LOU
(grabs Candy)
Come on, Candy.

CANDY
No. Let go of me, Lou Dimes.

(LOU pulls CANDY away from MATHU.)

CANDY
MATHU! MATHU! THIS PLACE IS GONNA DIE WITHOUT YOU. ITS NOTHING WITHOUT YOU!

(BLACKOUT. END OF SCENE THREE.)

ACT TWO

SCENE FOUR

SETTING: Tee Jack's Bar

AT RISE: It's evening at Tee Jack's Bar, Tee Jack, bar owner, cleaning the glasses. JACK MARSHALL enters.

TEE JACK
Hey! How are you, Jack?

(JACK MARSHALL tips his hat at TEE JACK. JACK sits on the barstool.)

TEE JACK
What can I get you?

JACK MARSHALL
Jack Daniels on the rocks.

TEE JACK
Sure thing, Jack. Daniels on the rocks coming up.

(TEE JACK puts ice on the glass and pours the Jack Daniels.)

JACK MARSHALL
Got to move on. Having supper with some of the boys in town. You sure you don't want to put a little bet on the game?

(TEE JACK hands the drink to JACK MARSHALL.)

TEE JACK
Don't like to take money from a new customer.

(JACK MARSHALL takes the drink.)

JACK MARSHALL
Better pray nothing to happen to Salt or Pepper.

(JACK MARSHALL finishes his drink. The glass is empty. He shows TEE JACK his empty glass.)

TEE JACK
(pours another)
Here you go, Jack. On the house.

JACK MARSHALL
Thanks.

(JACK MARSHALL sips his drink.)

JACK MARSHALL
You heard what happened to Beau?

TEE JACK
What about him?

JACK MARSHALL
Got himself killed.

TEE JACK
Beau's dead!

JACK MARSHALL
Mhmm.

TEE JACK
Holy shit. How did that happen? Where? When?

JACK MARSHALL
On that plantation.

TEE JACK
Is that true?

JACK MARSHALL
Mhmm. Mapes is down there getting some answers.

TEE JACK
Boy, boy, boy, we haven't had a good stringing in these parts in quite a while. We'll have one now, if you know Fix.

(LUKE WILL and his Men: HENRY, SHARP, LEROY, ROBERT and ALCEE enter.)

LUKE WILL
Gentlemen!

TEE JACK
Hey! How doin' guys? What can I get you?

LUKE WILL
Bring us some Cokes.

TEE JACK
No beer tonight, boys?

LUKE WILL
Just bring a bottle.

TEE JACK
You got it.

(TEE JACK gets their drinks.)

LUKE WILL
Mr. Marshall, how you doing?

(JACK MARSHALL tips his hat at LUKE WILL.)

LUKE WILL
Had some trouble I hear?

JACK MARSHALL
I didn't have any.

(JACK drinks his drink and looks away from LUKE WILL.)

LUKE WILL
That thing with Beau.

JACK MARSHALL
I heard he got himself killed.

LUKE WILL
One of your niggers did it, Mr. Marshall.

JACK MARSHALL
I ain't got no niggers. Never had any. Never will. They belong to her.

LUKE WILL
Where is Candy?

JACK MARSHALL
Down at the quarters I believe.

LUKE WILL
Oh, she still over there protecting her niggers?

JACK MARSHALL
I have no idea what's she is doing.

LUKE WILL
Is Mapes still down there playing detective?

JACK MARSHALL
From what I hear he is. Now if you don't mind, I would like to finish my drink.

(JACK ignores and drinks his drink.)

LUKE WILL
Another second of your time, Mr. Marshall.

(TEE JACK hands LUKE WILL and his Men the drinks.)

LUKE WILL
Alright let's toast. To our friend, Beau, we'll miss you.
(raise his drink)
To Beau.

MEN
(raise their drinks)
To Beau!

(LUKE WILL and his Men toast their drinks and takes a sip.)

LUKE WILL
You know what I think. I think Mapes needs help.

(JACK glance at LUKE WILL.)

LUKE WILL
I hope you wouldn't mind.

JACK MARSHALL
Are you suggesting I go down there and help him?

LUKE WILL
Not exactly.

JACK MARSHALL
What are you suggesting?

ROBERT
(light his cigarette)
Law seems to work slow at times.

SHARP
The old man ain't showing up.

LUKE WILL
His All-American son talked him out of it.

TEE JACK
That's a lie.

LUKE WILL
What's that you said, Tee Jack?

TEE JACK
I didn't mean it. God in Heaven knows I didn't mean that. Just slipped out, hearing that Fix wasn't coming here tonight. Just slipped out.

LUKE WILL
Careful, Tee Jack, my fuse is short.

TEE JACK
I can see why. Listen why don't you boys just have a bottle on me? All right?

LUKE WILL
(smiles)
Now you're talking, Tee Jack.

(LUKE WILL and his Men cheered and start drinking. ROBERT hands LUKE WILL a cigarette. LUKE WILL puts it in his mouth, ROBERT helps him lit it and He smokes it.)

ROBERT
So Fix's leaving it up to Mapes, huh?

LUKE WILL
It's not him. It's All-American fart and that hog-gut salesman there in Bayonne. They the ones talked him out of it. He wanted to come, but he wouldn't come without them. I left him there crying.

(TEE JACK takes LUKE WILL's cigarette and then he smokes it.)

TEE JACK
(blows a smoke)
My God! What's the world coming to?

LUKE WILL
The End. That's what it's coming to.

(JACK MARSHALL finishes his drink and gets up.)

JACK MARSHALL
Tee Jack, thank you for the drink.

TEE JACK
Jack, leaving us soon?

JACK MARSHALL
Yes.

ROBERT
Sir? Don't you own that place?

JACK MARSHALL
What place?

ROBERT
Where Beau was killed.

JACK MARSHALL
I own a third of it.

ROBERT
Don't you think you ought to do something?

JACK MARSHALL
The law is down there. That's what they pay him for.

TEE JACK
Have a good night Jack.

(JACK MARSHALL tips his hat at TEE JACK and he exits.)

LUKE WILL
(to Tee Jack)
Give us more bottles, Tee Jack.

TEE JACK
Sure boys sure.

(TEE JACK gets more bottles.)

LUKE WILL
You boys think they're doing the right thing? Taking the law in its own hands?

SHARP
Well the law is the law.

LUKE WILL
What law? Shit, I should run this law. A law that should niggers stay out of our land. Away from our families. Away from our children. Besides if it wasn't for us, any nigger will come shoot and get away with it.

GRIFFIN
(on the police radio)
This is Griffin here. Can anybody hear me over? I think we got a something going on down here.

(TEE JACK and everybody in the bar remain silent and hears GRIFFIN over the radio.)

GRIFFIN
(on the police radio)
I tried to tell Mapes, he wouldn't listen. Eighteen men with shotguns and he's been in there for fifteen minutes. We're gonna need a code three right away. Call stat-

(The radio cuts off.)

LUKE WILL
Aw, come on.

TEE JACK
God Dammit.

(TEE JACK tries to turn the knob and taps on the radio.)

TEE JACK
(turns off)
Damn radio.

LUKE WILL
You know what I think. I think Mapes is down there being soft with those old niggers. He's trying to let them get away. When's Mapes ever been our side?

LEROY
Yeah, you know what I think we should pay Marshall a visit. What do you say guys?

HENRY
I say we go to Marshall and kick some booty.

ALCEE
I hear that.

SHARP
Y'all just crazy.

HENRY
Crazy?

SHARP
Yeah, go on to Marshall, just go after those old men with guns.

LEROY
Whatchu mean? You scared Sharp? Scared of old men with guns.

SHARP

Scared? I ain't scared nothing. Maybe Gil is right. Times aren't what they used to be. I got wife and kids waiting for me back home. If I go to jail, who's gonna watch them? If I die right now, who's gonna be there for them, Luke? You?

LUKE WILL

A nigger killed Beau. And we're gonna let that slide? What are we gonna slide next? When one of them rapes your wife?

(SHARP stands up.)

SHARP

You know what I'm not drinking with you. Cause if a man was smart, he wouldn't want a war.

SHARP

(to Robert)

Robert are you with me?

ROBERT

(stands up)

Yeah, I don't want none this. I'm going home.

SHARP

And Luke Will if I were you. I would listen to his All-American son. That's what I would do.

(ROBERT and SHARP exit.)

LUKE WILL

(to Henry, Leroy, Alcee)

Any of y'all following along? Huh?

(HENRY, LEROY, and, ALCEE say nothing.)

LUKE WILL

That's what I thought.

LEROY

Forget them Luke. They're just scared to kill a bunch of negros.

LUKE WILL

Yeah whatever.

(LUKE WILL drinks his last bottle.)

LUKE WILL

Come on, let's get out of here.

(LUKE WILL and his MEN exit. BLACKOUT.END OF SCENE FOUR.)

ACT TWO

SCENE FIVE

SETTING: Outside of Mathu's House

AT RISE: JOHNNY PAUL and CLATOO enter.

JOHNNY PAUL

I can't believe what you are saying.

CLATOO

Well what we gonna do? Can't you see the man's patient done run out.

JOHNNY PAUL

If Mathu go to jail, we go, too. Ain't that's what we said?

CLATOO

Now listen, you know I care for Mathu. I love Mathu. He's like my brother. I'd do anything for this man.

(All the OLD Men including MATHU enter.)

MATHU

There ain't nothing to prove any more. Y'all done already proved it. I never thought I woulda seen this day. No, I never thought I woulda seen this day. Rooster with a gun, Red with a gun, Mat, Chimley, Billy. Never thought I would seen this day. Till a few minutes ago, I felt the same way that man out there feel about y'all never would 'mount to anything. But I was wrong. And he's still wrong. And I thank y'all. I'm proud of what I have become. I'm proud to be an African. You know why I'm proud to be an African? Cause they won't let me be a citizen here in this country. Hate them 'cause they hated y'all 'cause you never tried. Just a mean-hearted old man. All I ever been, till this hour.

MATHU

Clatoo is right. Y'all need to go home. I got to do what I got to do. Do what you can with all this old junk around here.

(MAPES and GRIFFIN enters.)

MAPES

Well I see everything is taken care of.

MATHU
Sheriff.

MAPES
Ready?

MATHU
(nods)
Yeah.

CHARLIE (O.S)
Mathu wait!

(MATHU stops. Everybody looks to find the familiar voice. CHARLIE enters.)

CHARLIE
You don't have to go nowhere.

(Everybody glances at CHARLIE.)

CHARLIE
(to Mapes)
Sheriff.

(CHARLIE comes toward MAPES.)

CHARLIE
Mathu, didn't do it. I did it Sheriff.

MAPES
Did what?

CHARLIE
I kilt Beau.

MAPES
Oh Dammit, Charlie. Not you.

CHARLIE
No, it was me. I'm the one who killed Beau Boutan. Not Mathu.

MAPES
Did Candy set you up?

CHARLIE
No Sheriff. Just me. Candy didn't do anything. I'm the one.

CHARLIE (CONT'D)
I'm a man Sheriff. I want the whole world to know I'm a man. A man ready to take on selfless responsibilities.

MAPES

Ok tell me about it Charlie.

CHARLIE

Yessir. And please sir call me "Mr. Biggs" sir. I call Candy "Miss Candy". So I suggest you call me "Mr. Biggs".

(LOU and CANDY enter.)

MAPES

Ok, tell me about it, Cha-. I mean Mr. Biggs. Start from the beginning, back there in the field.

CHARLIE

It didn't start back there in the field, Sheriff. It started fifty years ago. No, not fifty, more forty-fou-forty-five years ago. I'm fifty now. I'm sure I musta run when I was no more than five, 'cause I know Parrain was beating me for running when I was six. You remember the first time you beat me for running, Parrain? All my life. That's all I ever done in my life. Running. From black, From white, From nigger, From Cajun, both. All my life. Made me do what they wanted to do and 'bused me if I did it right or if I did it wrong. Just to 'buse me. And long as I was Big Charlie, nigger boy, I took it. But they come a day! There comes a day when a man must be a man. Not afraid of their shadow. I was doing my work good until Beau started cussing at me. I told him, "Hey, you ain't got to cuss at me like that!" He would beat me. I told him no. I told him I was quitting. I jumped down from the loader. I was on my way home. He got down off that tractor and came at me with a stalka cane. I grabbed me one too. I don't know why I did it. He started laughing, thinking I would never hit him and I did it. He came at me, and I hit back. I ran through the fields, Beau hopped on the tractor, this time chasing me with a shotgun. I tried screaming for help, no one came to me. He kept on screaming, saying, "I'm gonna get you Charlie boy." I ran I ran until I made at Parrain's house.

(CHARLIE looks at MAPES.)

MAPES

Go on!

(CHARLIE continues.)

CHARLIE (CONT'D)
He raised his gun. I pulled the trigger. After I pulled trigger, I saw Beau dead. I told Parrain I was scared. I told him I was go'n run and try to reach North. I told him they were bound to put me in the electric chair. I told him he had to say he did it, 'cause they didn't put people old as him in the electric chair. I told him Candy would protect him no matter what. So I lay the gun here and I ran I ran and I ran as fast as I could. Sometime 'round sundown I heard a voice calling my name. I laid there listening, listening and listening until I didn't hear it any more. But I knowed that voice was calling me back here.

MAPES
All right I believe you.

CHARLIE
I'm ready to go Sheriff.

(A sound of a car horn honking.)

MAPES
Shit, I don't believe this.

MAPES
(to Old Men and Charlie)
Let me handle this.

CHARLIE
This is my fight. He come here to lynch me, not you.

CLATOO
This everybody fights. Ain't nobody gonna be lynching here tonight.

MAPES
Y'all stay back.

LUKE WILL
SHERIFF! SHERIFF!

MAPES
Luke Will, go on home!

LUKE WILL
Bring that nigger out here and I'll go home.

MAPES
Griffin, get them out of here.

GRIFFIN
(taking off his belt)
No, Sheriff. I ain't raising my hand against no white folks for no niggers.

(GRIFFIN drops the belt and exit.)

MAPES
Griffin, you son of b-

(MAPES glance at LUKE WILL and his Men. He says nothing to them.)

MAPES
Come on, Mr. Biggs.

(CHARLIE glance at the Old Men one last time including MATHU and CANDY. He salutes them.)

CHARLIE
Here I come, Sheriff.

(CHARLIE follows MAPES. He gives a menace look at LUKE WILL and his Men. CHARLIE leaves with a black power fist in the air. CHARLIE and MAPES exit. A sound of siren and car leaving. LUKE WILL and his Men watch them leave then turns around at the OLD MEN.)

LUKE WILL
Well, what y'all gonna do huh? I ain't scared no fucking old black gizzards like all y'all.

(All the OLD MEN grab their guns, lock and loads their guns, aims their guns at LUKE WILL and his Men. CANDY and LOU take SNOOKUM away from the scene and hide behind the house.)

LUKE WILL
WHAT ARE WAITING FOR? THEY WANT A FIGHT! SHOOT THEM!!

LEROY
ARE YOU CRAZY??? THEY ALL GOT SHOT GUNS!!

(GABLE fired shots at them. LUKE WILL and his friends jumped. He missed.)

LUKE WILL
COME ON! SHOOT THEM!

(LEROY tries to aim. The OLD MEN shoot again. They scurry exit.)

MATHU

(stops the Old Men)

HOLD IT!! HOLD IT!!

(The OLD MEN stopped shooting. MATHU comes face to face with LUKE WILL points his gun at him.)

MATHU

(pointing the gun at Luke Will)

Luke Will go 'on home. No more setting foot in this plantation. Ain't nobody gonna be lynching tonight. Stay away from Marshall and Don't comeback.

(LUKE WILL stares at MATHU gun, pins his head at it, pushes it away and backs away from it.)

LUKE WILL

I'LL BE BACK! I'LL BE BACK!! I'LL COME FOR ALL OF YOU!

(LUKE WILL exit.)

MAT

We did it. Lord have mercy we did it.

(The OLD MEN cheered. MAT and CHIMLEY fired two shots in the air. Everybody hugs, holler, dance and shake hands in celebration. BLACKOUT. END OF SCENE FIVE.)

ACT TWO

SCENE SIX

SETTING: Camp site

AT RISE: Several months later, CANDY MARSHALL and LOU DIMES sitting by the fire covered with a blanket and holding each other.

LOU
This is nice, isn't it?

CANDY
(gloomy)
Yes it is.

(LOU sees CANDY upset.)

LOU
Come on Candy. I bought you out here just to cheer you up.

CANDY
I know.

LOU
Then what's wrong?

CANDY
Nothing.

LOU
Ok.

CANDY
Just can't believe Charlie is gone.

LOU
Yeah, me either. At least he owned up to the Sheriff. Look on the Brightside, Luke Will is dead after that deadly shootout.

CANDY
Yea, I know. Thank god. That asshole.

LOU
And to think I was the biggest asshole.

CANDY
Shut up!

(They laugh.)

CANDY
Musta think I'm stupid. Do you?

LOU
Nope, not at all.

(They were silence for a second.)

CANDY
I'm gonna miss Mathu.

LOU
I know, but he'll comeback.

CANDY
You really think so?

LOU
Of course. Maybe soon. But you know you can't protect that old man forever. Who knows?

LOU (CONT'D)
Maybe you don't know it. But after tonight there's going to be a big change in your life. That old man is now free from you. He doesn't need you to protect him.

(CANDY glance at LOU DIMES.)

CANDY
Why is that? What do you mean?

LOU
Before I leave here tonight, I want a yes or no to where our relationship is going. If I don't get any answer at all, I won't be coming back here anymore.

CANDY
You bastard.

LOU
That's possible. I wasn't there. But after tonight…

(CANDY slaps LOU. CANDY turns away, not looking at LOU.)

LOU
(rubbing his face)
That's how you feel?

(CANDY says nothing.)

LOU
Wow.

(LOU stands up.)

LOU
Always play too much. Gosh, Candy, you're always playing while I'm the one trying to be serious. You can ignore me all you want but I'm the one is trying to get close with you.

LOU (CONT'D)
All I want is you. You in my life forever. To be my everything, to be the mother of my children, to be my life. My wife. Isn't that too hard to ask, Candy?

(CANDY grabs LOU'S face and kisses him.)

LOU
I'm guessing that's a yes, huh?

(CANDY smiles. They continued kissing. FADE TO BLACK. END OF ACT TWO.)

CURTAIN CALL

Made in United States
Orlando, FL
18 February 2022